THE ELOCUTION OF BENJAMIN FRANKLIN

BY steve j. spears

CURRENCY PRESS
The performing arts publisher

GRIFFIN THEATRE COMPANY

CURRENT THEATRE SERIES

First published in 1989
by Currency Press Pty Ltd,
Gadigal Land, Suite 310, 46–56 Kippax Street, Surry Hills, NSW 2010, Australia
enquiries@currency.com.au
www.currency.com.au

This edition first published in 2026 by Currency Press in association with Griffin Theatre Company

Typeset by Brighton Gray for Currency Press.
Printed by Fineline Print + Copy Services, Revesby, NSW.
Cover image by Daniel Boud. Cover design by Susu Studio.

Currency Press acknowledges the Traditional Owners of the Country on which we live and work. We pay our respects to all Aboriginal and Torres Strait Islander Elders, past and present.

A catalogue record for this book is available from the National Library of Australia

Contents

The Elocution of Benjamin Franklin was first performed at the Nimrod Theatre, Gadigal Country, Sydney, on 28 August 1976 with the following cast:

MAN	Gordon Chater

Director, Richard Wherrett
Set Designer, Larry Eastwood

CHARACTERS

MAN. Jovial, fat and fiftyish

SETTING

ACT ONE

The present. A house in Double Bay.

ACT TWO

The same.

ACT THREE

Eight years later. A mental hospital.

AUTHOR'S NOTE

The word 'Blink' which is used in the stage directions indicates a lighting change to represent the passing of time. The length of these passages varies from a few seconds to several days. Most often, the blinks are quick lights-off/lights-on blackouts—but the word also serves as shorthand for cross-fades, cross-snaps and longer blackouts. My thanks to Richard Wherrett for coining the term.

Steve J. Spears, 1977

ACT ONE

A living room cum studio in a small house in Double Bay.

A door at prompt leads to the hall, the front door and the bedroom. A door at opposite prompt (OP) leads to the bathroom and, farther on, to the kitchen.

Furniture includes a piano, a telephone table with an ornate lamp, a roll-top desk, a bust of Shakespeare prominently displayed, some comfortable chairs, a coffee table, a cuckoo clock, and a shotgun mounted over the fireplace. An electric heater is on in the fireplace.

There is a bay window at the back with the words 'SHAKESPEARE SPEECH AND DRAMA' lettered on it.

The Venetian blinds on this window are open, and the morning sun streams through.

MONDAY 1ST

The MAN *enters, naked, a bath towel over his shoulder, whistling. He is jovial, fat and fiftyish.*

He rolls up the roll-top desk, takes out a make-up case and mirror and begins quickly and expertly to apply rouge and other make-up. During this, he turns on the record player: the music is the Skyhooks' 'Ego is not a Dirty Word'.

He finishes making up, takes out a large, battered poster of Mick Jagger and sticks it on the wall.

He wraps the towel around him, turns off the record player, takes a pair of black leather gloves from the roll-top, puts them on and stands in front of the poster. He begins to caress himself, then stops.

He turns the bust of Shakespeare away and stands in front of the poster again.

MAN: [*in a girlish voice*] Yes, Mick. I … I thought so too. Ooooooo, it's such an honour to meet you, Mick. Yes, I was at the show. I thought you were fabulous. Keith too, I think you're both dreamy. Oooooo. Yes. You like my gloves, Mick? They're very sensuous, don't you think? Hmmm. They feel smooth. Yes. Smooth. Hmmm.

The telephone rings.

Shit!

He strides purposefully to the telephone, calling to it as he moves.

Shut up! [*To Mick Jagger*] Excuse me.

[*Picking up the telephone*] Good morning. Shakespeare Speech and Drama Academy … Yes. This is he. Yes, Mrs Franklin?

Pause.

Yes … I dare say. Oh. Yes, stuttering can be painful, absolutely painful. Especially for a twelve-year-old … Oh, that's so unnecessary for the little man, Mrs Franklin. Aren't children cruel? Well, I'd certainly like to try to help him, Mrs Franklin. Unless it's something physical, these problems can be overcome. You see, good speech is as much an art as music or painting. Correct speech is not accidental … Yes. Yes. Certainly, today would be fine.

Making a 'shit' face.

This morning?

Making another 'shit' face.

Well, um …

He looks through his notebook.

Shall we say eleven?

Fine. Fine. Don't worry, Mrs Franklin, we'll have that stutter licked before you can say 'Susan stole thirty-three thistle sticks'. Hahahahaha … Well, my fee is eight dollars per half-hour lesson. Very well. Yes, we'll see you and little Benjamin at eleven. Yes. Bye-bye, Mrs Franklin.

He hangs up and speaks to the poster.

Well, Michael, I'm sorry, but we've got another stutterer.

He takes the poster from the wall.

Anyway, don't you think you're getting a bit old for this sort of thing?

He puts the poster, make-up, gloves and mirror away.

Benjamin Franklin. Ughhh.

[*Turning Shakespeare bust around*] Tell me, William, if your last name happened to be 'Franklin', what sort of person would you have to be to name your son Benjamin? Hmmm? A fuckwit, that's what. God, there's some weird people in the world. Well, I don't know about you, but I'm going to put some clothes on.

[*Fingering the rouge*] And I suppose I'd better get this stuff off too … Why, thank you.

[*Pinching the bust's cheek*] You too.

MAN *exits. We hear running water and blubbering. He peeks into the room with a wet face.*

All better.

MAN *trips across the stage singing 'Ego is not a dirty word', playfully flashes himself at bust and exits. He speaks offstage.*

I think the checked pants and the maroon shirt today. Oh, my god!

MAN *enters, wearing old-fashioned underpants and singlet, and storms across the stage.*

Guess who forgot to brush their teeth?

MAN *places hand in front of mouth and breathes hard. He makes a disgusted noise and exits, OP. We hear running water and a garbled chant.*

Thirty strokes up and down, thirty strokes round and round. Do it proper, do it right and you'll have teeth all clean and bright.

Spit!

Gargle.

MAN *springs into the room, singing 'How's your love life?', and prepares to exit.*

Telephone rings.

He does a military 'about face'.

Shakespeare Speech and Drama. Bruce! How nice. Why, you filthy animal … Listen, I can't talk, I've got someone coming … No, stupid, a new pupil. Listen, pet, you take them when you can get them at eight bucks a pop. Didn't bat a vocal organ. They never do. Not in Double Bay, pet … It's a young boy who stutters. They're my specialty. No, Bruce. Stutterers! Oh, you'll like this. The mother's name is Franklin. Guess what they named the poor kid … [*Bitterly*] God, you're a bore, Bruce. Yes. Top marks. Uh-huh. Eleven o'clock. What's the time? Shit! I must go. They probably won't come. If you knew how many stutterers and stammerers and mumblers and toneless monotonous nasal voices ring up and solemnly assure me, yes, they really want to improve their diction and, yes, I'll be there, and then disappear into that inarticulate void at the other end of the phone without showing their tonsils … Bruce, I'm going. Goodbye, I'm half-naked and … No, I don't plan to greet them naked. And I don't plan to greet them in my lounging outfit. No, come eleven, they'll be greeted by the most masculine Aussie since Bob—

He spits.

Hawke … Oh Bruce, he is not. Fuck you. Goodbye. What? No. Not tonight, love. I've got classes till—

He consults his notebook.

—ten. Hmmm. Then I thought I'd just go to bed with Mick Jagger. Never mind. I'll ring you.

He looks at his watch.

Shit! Bye-bye.

MAN *exits. We hear him grunting and getting dressed.*

The doorbell rings.

He calls from offstage.

Just a minute.

MAN *enters, clambering into shoes. The doorbell rings.*

Just a minute.

Blink.

MAN *is revealed sitting in a spot.*

Yes, Mrs Franklin. Feel free to smoke if you wish. You'll find the ashtray there. No smoking for you, though, Benjamin. Hahaha. Just a joke, Mrs, er, Franklin. I must congratulate you on your choice of a name for your son. Very imaginative and a fine name too. Well, Benjamin. Not many people know this, but when I was your age, I used to stutter too. Yes. And oh dear, it was much worse than yours. And the other kids used to make fun of me. They do the same to you, do they? It's not very nice, is it? They used to call me Tommy-gun. But, believe me, it's not worth worrying about what other kids say. You should just tell them to get … lost. Anyway, do you know what we're going to do? Hmmmmm? We're going to stop you stuttering once and for all. I could do it in ten minutes, but I want your mum's money. Hahaha. Just a joke, Mrs, er, Franklin. So, we'll take a bit longer than that. How old are you? … [*Smiling*] That's alright. I know how tough those T's are, and the P's. Hmmmmm?

He winks reassuringly.

Well, Ben, would you wait outside? I'd like to talk to Mum.

He watches him leave.

Beautiful boy. Mrs Franklin, you're to be congratulated again. For bringing your son here, or to any speech therapy school for that matter. People go through life crippled by [*tapping throat and face*] just six inches of their body, by an inability to communicate and then refusing, stupidly refusing to seek help. Help is what I offer. We won't consider today's little get-together a lesson, I think, er, tomorrow? Right.

He jots it down in his notebook.

We'll start him off tomorrow then with a ten-week course every Tuesday at four? Fine. Certainly, in advance, if you'd care to. I think I might throw in a few drama lessons, too. Who knows? Once the stutter's gone, we might have a budding Frank Thring on our hands. No. On second thoughts, Frank's rather poor on his S's. Hahahaha. Oh, and the lessons are private of course, and I do prefer if parents aren't in the room, it makes them shy, you understand. And I'm afraid I don't have a waiting room, so if you do drive him here, you will have to wait in your car. Most uncivilised, I know, but I hope you'll forgive me.

[*Taking the cheque*] Thanks so much. We'll see young Benjamin at four sharp tomorrow. Fine. [*Getting up*] I'll see you to the door.

Blink.

The cuckoo clock strikes ten.

It is night outside the windows.

MAN *is at front door, OP.*

Yes. Bye-bye, Mrs Clifton.

MAN *closes the door and slumps wearily.*

Please God, don't let me have any lessons in the morning.

He consults his notebook and grimaces.

Diana South, the lisping chemist, the pharmaceutical sibilant stomper, you have made a hole in my morning. [*Evilly*] Why don't you quit, you thilly apothecary? You know, you never do your exercises. [*To bust*] William, if I pray hard enough, Diana South will pick up her phone in her hideous high-rise, she'll ring me up, apologise for the lateness of the hour and quit. Help me.

He adopts an attitude of prayer.

The telephone rings. He answers it smugly.

Yes, Diana? Bruce? … No, I thought … never mind. I keep forgetting I'm an atheist. Hmmmm? I know I'm not making sense. I've just spent eleven hours servicing the soft and hard palates of half of Sydney … I'd love you to come over in the morning, pet. I was just trying to arrange it with [*pointing up*] Jehovah, but … I've got the whole morning free except for a pupil right smack dab in the middle of the a.m. Ten-thirty. Have you? Look, I'd love to see them, Bruce, but … No. You may not hide in my bedroom. You aren't to get near my pupils, capisce? That would be all I need, one of the mums to see a six-foot-two lady with a five o'clock shadow playing skippy with their favourite eight-year-old.

Pause.

Look, I'm sorry, Bruce. I didn't mean to offend you, but you know that I must keep the school completely divorced from this twilight world in which I move.

Pause.

Bruce! Don't over-react! Look, love, I'm fucked. Please let me go to bed. What about tomorrow night? Hmmm? Seven-thirty. I'll cook something. Alright? Bye-bye.

[*Putting down the telephone*] Miss South! This is your conscience speaking. You like your lisp! It's cute! Men find it fetching! It goes with your blonde hair and your blue eyes! Ring me! Quit! Let me sleep in!

Silence. MAN *prepares to exit, P.*

The telephone rings.

Hello? Miss South?

Pause.

No, that's alright. You're what? Oh, that is a shame. No, I understand. You're sure now? Very well. To tell you the truth, Diana, all you have to do is practise those exercises every day and your lisp will [*snapping his fingers*] poof! Oh, your new boyfriend likes it? He says it goes with your blonde hair and blue eyes, does he? Hahaha. Well, my dear. As an elocution teacher I'm appalled, but as an unabashed romantic, you have my blessings. Lisp on, honey. Yes. And if you meet anyone special who doesn't like it, well, give me a call. Bye-bye, dear. Best of luck. Yes. Bye.

He hangs up.

He kisses bust and looks quizzically to heaven.

He takes poster and leather gloves out of a roll-top desk and moves off, P.

Come on, Mick, I'm horny.
'Over one arm the lusty courser's rein,
Under the other was the tender boy.'

He exits.

'Who blushed and pouted in dull disdain.' Hehehehehe.

Silence.

My God!

He speaks in a garbled voice offstage.

Thirty strokes up and down, thirty strokes round and round. Do it proper, do it right and you'll have teeth all clean and bright.

Spit!

Blink.

TUESDAY 2ND

MAN: [*sitting in spot*] Well, Benjamin. Is your mum waiting outside? Fine. We'll be having lessons for the next ten weeks. Don't tell your mum, but we'll piss that stutter off in three weeks, then we'll get onto something really interesting.

He lights a cigar.

You move well, Benjamin, and there's something in your voice I like. I've got a feeling there's an actor inside you. I guess you never go into school plays or whatnot? Huh?

He lights a match.

He makes an explosive P that blows out the match.

Here.

[*Tossing 'Ben' the matches*] Light one of those up and go Puh!

That's right.

That's good.

Do it again.

Sure. Do it again.

[*Wryly*] Fun, isn't it?

Hmmmm?

Menthol or plain?

There's a packet on the piano. Don't you tell your mum or I'll put you over my knee.

Sit down. Breathe. Just breathe. Nice big one.

Bigger.

Bigger.

Did you notice then, when you took a deep breath you filled up here?

[*Tapping his chest*] This time try it differently, feel around.

Come here. Feel around the bottom of my rib cage just here.

Yes, that's right. When I breathe you notice that I fill up down there. That's the diaphragm. That's where you have to fill up. Can you feel that?

Okay. Now squiggle your hands down round your hips and feel around for your diaphragm. Think your breath down there. Let me feel.

He puts out his hands with a look of concentration.

Hmmmm. Again.

Again.

Great. Okay. Good. This time really take it down there and say:

[*Singing*] Bell, bell, bell, bell, bell.

Try it. Come on. Don't be shy with me. Bell, bell, bell, bell, bell.

Come on, Benjamin. You are shy, aren't you? Listen, if I can sit here making a fool of myself, then you can too. Alright? I'll let you keep the packet. Okay? Okay. Off you go.

Good, Ben. Good. Now relax, unwind, breathe down in your diaphragm and do it again. Beautiful. I'll give you two packets. Now.

Relax. Sit down. Have a smoke. Let me tell you about speech. Breath is the basis of all speech. Breath. Fill your diaphragm with enough breath and you can shake the window and rattle the walls. You can count to a hundred without pausing. Watch.

MAN *starts counting slowly and distinctly. He reaches sixty or seventy and grins shyly.*

See? You'll be doing that soon. Anyway, breath. Breath. Breath passes up to the voice box, which has two vocal chords, a big one and a little one, and the breath causes them to vibrate, just like a guitar string. This sound is then made into speech by teeth, nasal cavities, tongue and all sorts of stuff in your mouth. So that instead of going, 'woof, woof', we can go, 'Benjamin, if you must smoke, use an ashtray.' Now your problem is that you aren't breathing correctly and your speech muscles aren't performing properly. It's a bit complicated, but it's certainly nothing to worry about and it's nothing to be ashamed of. It's just … there. Like … pimples. Okay. Now, next week when you come back, I want to hear you saying the bells with a nice rich forward tone. There's a rainbow from your mouth to mine and you're going to send it out, up and over. Bell, bell, bell. And I want to hear you counting slowly and distinctly up to thirty. And I bet you won't be able to. Okay? That's all. You're doing well, Benjamin. See, it doesn't hurt much, does it? Now, what do you normally do after school?

Slow fade. Cuckoo clock strikes six.

Lights fade up. Night time. MAN *is at front door, OP.*

Bye, Mr Teifvle.

He closes door, stretches, saunters over to piano and plays 'My Dog Has Fleas' and 'Chopsticks', badly.

He reaches behind piano, pulls out bottle of whisky and takes a swig.

He burps genteelly.

Exits.

My God!

MAN *enters, tense. He is wearing knickers and a stuffed bra.*

Hit the deck, boys.

He falls to the ground, impersonating a marine.

Okay, youse guys, lizzen. See dat winda over there? Luxaflex's open, see? It's supposed to be shut, see? We got orders. Ain't no-one supposed to see me, get it? Ain't no-one supposed to look through de winda, see? And see me knickers, see? Okay. Let's go.

Dramatic war music. MAN *inches his way across the room, past the piano. Finally, dramatically, he closes the blind and draws the curtain.*

He stands, exhausted but victorious, and looks proudly at his men.

You did alright, boys.

MAN *starts to stagger off, P, then re-enters, putting on fluffy dressing gown.*

Blink.

MAN *is revealed in a spot, sipping tea daintily.*

Let me bore you for a minute, Bruce. Remember I was telling you about this boy who stutters? Benjamin Franklin? Oh, I told you about him. Jesus, Bruce, you never listen. Anyway, he's this beautiful, beautiful twelve-year-old boy who moves like a prince with this long, dark, curly hair. Well, Benjamin has this mother. [*Pulling a face*] The most rigid, humourless, clinging, tight-arsed bitch I've ever seen … apart from my ex-wife. And Benjamin is literally terrified of her. He had his first lesson today and good old Mum was waiting outside in her P76 like this—

He mimes a chain-smoker.

—and Ben kept glancing back through the window—

He mimes a paranoid glance.

—every thirty seconds on the second. I swear to Christ he had me doing it. I thought the old lady was going to come crashing through my window, waving a tyre jack, beat my brains out and effect a rescue. And she wonders why he stutters. Christ, I'm amazed he can talk!

He lights his cigar.

Hmmmm? What do you mean it spoils the atmosphere? Look, I got lace doilies, real china teacups.
[*Grabbing teapot*] Look! I even knitted this tea cosy.
[*Dramatic*] What do you want from me?
[*Grabbing bosom*] Milk? Yes, Bruce.

Pause.

Yes, Bruce.

He stubs out his cigar.

Better? Where was I? [*Enthusiastically*] Ah, Benjamin. Anyway, I carefully pointed out the miracle of Luxaflex blinds and gave him a cigarette—Oh, give me a cigarette will you, darling?—and just talked with him for a while.

Pause.

This kid's fucked more women than I have. He's going around with an older lady now. She's sixteen and works at Mum's hairdressing salon. And just for one minute … he didn't stutter. There was this twelve-year-old man of the world quietly sitting back, fag in mouth, telling me about what a great gobbler his mum's hairdresser is. Hahaha. Isn't that superb? And for that one minute … he didn't stutter.

Reflective pause.

Huh? Oh, knock it off Bruce. Okay. Bore me. How are your kids?

Clock strikes eleven.

He yawns.

Shit, I hate that clock. Can't think why I keep it. Come on, Bruce, time to turn back into a pumpkin. I'm for bed and you're for home, wife and kiddies.

Pause.

Bruce, I think your outfit's lovely and, to get terribly maudlin … I'm glad you're my friend. [*Defiantly*] Okay? Anyway, you're the best transvestite stockbroker I know. Get changed. I'll unzip you.

Blink.

WEDNESDAY 3RD

It is dawn.

MAN *sits watching the sunrise, smoking, mascara stains on his cheeks.*

The clock strikes six.

MAN *looks at it absently, moves to the piano and plays 'My Dog Has Fleas' and 'Chopsticks', badly, then closes it gently.*

He turns on lamp beside telephone and dials.

MAN: Hel … Hello. Service-phone? Yes, it's, er, Shakespeare Speech and Drama here. Would you, er, hang on?

[*Juggling notebook and phone*] Yes. Ready? Ring Jane Montgomery, Archie Duff, Ian Mauger. E-E? What's his name?—er, Eric Palegeorge, Kevin Richards, Margaret Sherlock, Len Teifvle—that's E.I.F.V.L.E—um, Mrs Jane Clifton and Georgina Van Hyphen Rees. Also send a messenger to Ms Maura Croghan, Five Beatty Avenue, Woollahra. Tell them all that the classes have been cancelled today. You know, be nice to them, apologise profusely and all that … tell them teacher's sick. Yes, it is getting to be a bit of a habit, isn't it? Are you the same girl who took my call last time? Tell me, have you ever thought of taking speech lessons? I'll do you wholesale. Hehe. Thanks very much. Oh, and take my calls today, will you? Bye-bye.

He exits. Bedroom light goes on.

Stop looking at me like that, William.

[*Slowly*] I am not cleaning my teeth. [*Disdainfully*] I am in bed and I am staying in bed, alright? Night-night.

Bedroom light goes off.

He sighs with satisfaction, then speaks hypnotically.

My feet are sleeping. My ankles are sleeping. My calves are sleeping. My thighs are sleeping. My … telephone lamp is still on. William! Turn off that lamp while you're out there.

Lamp goes out.

Thank you. My feet—

Silence. Bedroom light goes on.

MAN *enters.*

Am I going crazy or did you …?

Bust does not answer.

MAN *gingerly pulls the lamp switch off and on several times. Nothing happens.*

You old fraud.

He takes out the globe with a handkerchief.

I bet it was Bacon, you creep.

Clock strikes the half hour.

Shut up.

MAN *strides to telephone and dials.*

Hello, Service-phone? Oh hello, pet. 'Shakespeare' here. Still working? Have you rung any of those numbers yet? Good. Listen, forget it. Tear them up. Yes, it's getting to be quite a habit, isn't it? Sorry. What? Well you know, the show must go on and all that. Yes. Bye-bye.

MAN *puts down telephone, irritated with himself. He wearily exits, P.*

Blink.

Doorbell rings.

MAN *stands in a spot in masculine clothes.*

Naughty Nancy ate nine nice new cakes.

Pause.

That's good, Maura, but watch the 'noines' and the 'noises'. Again? … Maura? Have you been doing your exercises? Come on, 'fess up. I thought so. And all week I've had visions of Naughty Nancy gobbling up these nice new cakes and they haven't been touched! I don't suppose Fred and Frank have been fighting on Friday either? Hmmmmm? Tsk, tsk. What are you, a Muslim or a pacifist? Never mind, dear. This is the last time I'm letting you off the hook. Next time.

He runs a thumb across his throat.

From the top: 'Naughty Nancy ate nine nice new cakes.'

Blink.

MAN *appears in a spot.*

Inflections are the little glides of the voice up and down. When we glide upward, we call it the rising inflection? When we glide downward, we call it the falling inflection. The rising inflection is used when the meaning of a sentence is incomplete? Also, in questions where the answer can be given as yes or no? Do you understand? However, the falling inflection is used when the meaning of a sentence is complete, or in questions when the answer cannot be given as yes or no. What's your name?

Okay. Although the voice has many keys, we divide them, for convenience, into one: high; two: medium; and three: low.

Kevin, [*gloomily*] tell me what we use the low key for.

[*Sorrowfully*] Very good.

[*Excited*] Now quick! Tell me what we use the high key for. Quick! Quick!

[*Sympathetically*] Why, that's completely correct. Medium key we use for everyday conversation when we blabber on about what's happening and what the weather's like and what it's going to be like and so on but you'll notice when I speak like this in the same medium key without any rising inflections or falling inflections or changes of key or emphasis or pauses that it gets awfully boring boring boring.

Pause.

Doesn't it get boring? [*Laughing*] There's nothing worse is there?

Blink.

He appears in a spot again.

No, Georgina. Like this:

[*As Miss Barrett*] Oh, Mr Browning, your poems with their great-hearted acceptance of life, you cannot imagine what they mean to me. Here I am shut in my four walls, the view of Wimpole Street my only glimpse of the world, and those wonderful people out there of every age and country and all so tingling with life, life, life! No, you'll never know how much I owe you.

[*As Browning*] You … you … really mean that?

[*As Miss Barrett*] Why, Mr Browning.

[*As Browning, with cigar*] But of course you do, or you wouldn't have said it. What you say, Miss Barrett, makes up to me for all the cold-shouldering I've had to accept from the public.

[*As Miss Barrett*] It infuriates me. Sometimes I detest the British public.

[*As Browning, with cigar*] Hahahahahaha. Oh dear. No. Good old British public. Hahahahaha, mind you, Miss Barrett, I've an uneasy feeling that my style is largely to blame for my unpopularity.

[*As Miss Barrett*] Well, perhaps there are passages in your books that are a little involved. I have marked one or two here in your *Sordello* which rather puzzled me. Here for instance.

[*As Browning, with cigar*] Oh, *Sordello*. I've done my best to forget it. However, let me see.

He looks over Sordello.

Well, Miss Barrett, when I wrote *Sordello*, only God and Robert Browning knew what it meant. Now I'm afraid only God knows.

[*As himself*] See, Mrs Van-Rhys? You speak with the hands as much as the lips. Take it home again and practise Miss Barrett's part. And remember, think pale, washed out, ill and humble and you'll get it. That will do for today. I'll see you out.

MAN *exits.*

We hear front door, OP, being opened. Lights gradually come up.

Bye-bye, Mrs Van-Rhys. [*Waving*] Hello, Mrs Broad! [*Muttering*] Nosey bitch.

MAN *closes door.*

Clock strikes six.

There is still some light outside window.

MAN *reaches behind piano, takes out bottle of whisky and swigs.*

He walks with bottle to door OP and exits, swigging. He re-enters, swigging, with globe, and replaces globe in the lamp beside the telephone. He tries it a couple of times and swigs. He dials and swigs from the now-almost-empty bottle.

Oh, hello, Edith. How are you? Yes, I saw it last night. I think it suits him to a tee. No Edith, I thought the hemline was just right. Oh, you raised it yourself, did you? Why, that rotten bit—bastard told me he did it. Can—ooops—may I speak to him? Thanks. Oh, how are the kids? Great.

Pause.

Bruce, my pet, do you realise what a fine woman your wife is? Why don't you bring her over for one of our evenings? I've got some great recipes she'd love. Listen, I'm sorry to call you at home, but I wanted you to congratulate me. Because I thought that today was definitely the day that I wouldn't make it through and I did, that's why. Well, [*looking at bottle*] a bit. [*Swigging*] Come over, can you? You're taking her where? The (current state theatre company production)? Ah Bruce! I want to celebrate! Making it through today! Jesus, you never listen to me—alright. Take the bitch there. It's lousy! Yes, yes. Dominus vobiscum, creep.

[*Slamming down telephone*] Christ, it's hard being the other woman.

MAN *strides to darkening window.*

That's right, sun! Phoebus, you coward! Go on, desert me too, you cunt! Go and set! See if I care. But remember, Phoebus, when you come tomorrow, I'll still be here! You want to know why?

He gives the sky the finger.

Because, Phoeb, I got staying power! I got balls. And you can fucking set and—

Telephone rings.

MAN *strides to it, picks it up.*

What? Oh, Mrs Broad. You could hear me all the way over there? Heh. That's diaphragm breathing for you, does it every time. Tell me, have you ever thought of taking speech lessons, dear? Look, I'd love to talk some more, Mrs Broad, but I think I can smell my cake burning. Bye-bye.

He puts the telephone down and turns to the bust.

That was Mrs Broad. She thinks I'm a pervert. You know what I think. I think she does it with dogs. 'Sright.

He reaches behind the piano, brings out a portable TV.

'Sright. I think she's got a Dalmatian for a lover.

From the kitchen, he collects bread rolls, tins of food, cheese, fritz, can-openers, biscuits, etc. and heaps them on tray with TV.

And I think she's got her eye on that cute little dachshund down the road. And what's more, she's nosey.

MAN *strides to window and shouts:*

How's the bulldog these days? Huh! Up the mighty Roosters! Go, you big men! Come on! Go Russell, you little beauty! Wahooooooooooo. Get 'em in the nuts, Artie! Wahoooooooo.

The telephone rings. He picks it up, puts it down on table and exits with tray of food and TV set.

We hear squabbling from the telephone.

MAN *switches off main light, switches on bedroom light. Telephone lamp is left on. Bust looks unimpressed. We hear* MAN *rustling around in room and sounds of TV.*

END OF ACT ONE

ACT TWO

TUESDAY 9TH

It is raining outside the window.

Alarm clock sounds in bedroom and is shut off with a curse.

MAN *eventually emerges from P wrapped in his fluffy dressing gown, irritable. He exits, OP.*

We hear the shower running.

MAN *enters, trips, puts* Livin in the 70s *by Skyhooks on the record player and exits, OP.*

MAN *sings with record. It gets stuck on 'It's a horror movie right there ... ' (from 'Horror Movie').*

MAN *enters, irritable, dripping, and smashes record. He puts on another (Side One:* Let It Bleed *by Rolling Stones). He exits OP.*

MAN *sings with record. Shower noises finish.*

MAN *enters with towel wrapped around him. As he passes the record player, the needle slips and jumps.* MAN, *scarcely pausing, picks up record and smashes it, then exits P door.*

We hear towel-rubbing and grunting.

MAN *enters in undies and singlet, towelling his hair and exits OP to kitchen.*

We hear dishes rattling. One breaks.

MAN *enters with bowl of cornflakes, irritable. He moves to window, shovelling the cornflakes down.*

MAN: Good morning, Sydney. I see you've got another great day planned for me.

He spills some cornflakes on his singlet.

Yes.

He patiently pulls his singlet up and sucks them off. He turns to face the room, irritable, and looks ruefully around.

Huh.

MAN *exits to kitchen.*

We hear many dishes breaking.

Slowly MAN *enters, dignified.*

Blink.

MAN *appears in a spot.*

Emphasis! You can emphasise a word by making it [*loudly*] louder! Or [*softly*] by making the word softer. Or by pausing before or after the important—

Pause.

—word. Or by [*hysterically*] changing the key of the voice. Awe. That's A-W-E: 'What may this mean that thou dead corpse again in complete steel revisit'st thus the glimpses of the moon, making night hideous.' Anger: 'Back to thy punishment, false fugitive and to thy speed add wings! Lest with a whip of scorpions I pursue thee!' Ecstasy: 'Lend, lend your wings. I mount. I fly. O grave, where is thy victory? O death, where is thy sting?' See?

Blink.

MAN *appears in a spot.*

[*In a pirate voice*] You see that shotgun over the fireplace? There's an awful lot of dead little girls buried in my cellar who didn't practise 'Naughty Nancy ate nine nice new cakes'. Pow! Straight through the eyes. [*Normal voice*] I, er, hope it won't be necessary to take that gun down, Maura, I sincerely hope it won't be necessary. Let's hear you.

Blink.

MAN *appears in a spot.*

Tong tong tong a tong tong. That is the rhythm of the elephant's song.

Blink.

MAN *appears in a spot.*

Hark to the echo of London's old bells.

Blink.

He appears in a spot again.

Tip a tap tap. Tip a tap tap.

Blink.

He appears in a spotlight again.

But soft. What light, er, what light through yonder window breaks? It is …

Blink.

He appears in a spot.

Get it up your nose, Mrs Clifton.

Blink.

MAN *appears in a spot mouthing the numbers: 38, 39, 40, 41, 42.*

That's, um, that's great, Benjamin.

[*Tossing him a packet of cigarettes*] It's good that you're doing your exercises.

[*Eagerly*] How's the hairdresser?

Slow fade to black.

Laughter. Lights fade up.

MAN *is at telephone. It is darkening outside the window.*

Anyway, apparently, the hairdresser had the clap! Yes! And Benjamin had to sneak down to the VD Clinic after cricket on Saturday. Hahahaha. Then … then … he found out he … had crabs too! Hahahahaha. And his mum can't understand why he doesn't want to get his hair cut there anymore! Hahahahaha. See you tonight. Right, Bruce. Bye-bye.

MAN *puts down telephone.*

He starts laughing. Hooting, he exits P door. More laughter.

Lights fade into spot.

MAN *enters in fluffy dressing gown, sipping tea, and sits down in spot.*

I tell you, Bruce, this kid's a born actor. You should have been there when he was telling the story. You would have died, honestly.

Everything. The gestures, the faces. And his stutter: it's barely noticeable when he's really … giving out. His P's are still—

He makes a 'so-so' gesture.

—but he's coming along. After one week! I'm making history with this kid. I should get a write-up in the *Speech Therapy Gazette*. See, I think all he needs is a father figure. [*Sipping daintily*] His dad's always off somewhere, Singapore, America, you know. Hither and thither. And … oh … he counted up to forty-nine in one breath. That's incredible for anyone, let alone a twelve-year-old. Natural breath control. So, I want to crack that stutter and move on to drama. Honestly, with his looks and my talent, he could be great.

Pause.

I sound like a proud parent, don't I? As soon as I think he's ready, I'm going to get onto Healy at the ABC. They've got a series coming up that Benjamin would be ideal for. Yes. I might get into management. Fuck this elocution crap. Christ, I might even get back into the business. There's plenty of nice juicy roles for fat fifty-year-olds.

Pause.

In five years, Benjamin Franklin ...

He makes a distasteful face.

Benjamin Franklin. Benjamin Nicholas Franklin. Nicholas Franklin. Nicholas B. Franklin. Nick Franklin. Frank Nicholas. Ben Franklin. What do you think?

Pause.

Oh come off it, Bruce. If you can talk about that fucking Stock Exchange and your saintly martyred wife and those cretinous medical students with pimples you sired, then I can talk about my boy. Bruce. Listen. This kid is more than adequate. For the first time I feel like I can be more than adequate. I was an adequate actor, I'm an adequate teacher and an adequate man, I'm even just an adequate transvestite. Jesus, I can't even fantasise further than Mick Jagger. This kid can save me.

Pause.

Listen, you, [*sternly*] I want a bit of empathy and understanding from you or I'll bite your balls off, capisce? Okay. And if you're good, I'll wear that wig you bought me. [*Coaxing*] Come on, stop pouting. I'll buy your kids some Clearasil. Alright. My final offer. I'll go to the art gallery with you next Sunday all dressed up, how's that? Yes. Thought that would perk you up. Next Sunday. But you pay for a hotel room for us to change in. And since you're so rich, I want a room at the Sebel. Them's me conditions.

Pause.

And I'll never smoke cigars again and I'll call you Belinda when you're dressed up. You drive a hard bargain … Belinda.

Doorbell rings.

MAN *ignores it.*

Doorbell rings.

MAN *ignores it.*

Doorbell rings.

[*Whispering*] I hate not answering the door.

We hear footsteps outside window.

Shit! They're trying to peek in! I hope those Luxaflex … It might be a burglar!

MAN *takes off high-heeled shoe. We hear footsteps and window rattling.*

[*Whispering*] He's trying to get in! The window's not locked!

Silence.

Clock strikes nine very loudly.

MAN *is startled.*

Silence.

He's gone.

He picks up teacup rattlingly.

How about a real drink?

Pause.

We might have been raped!

Blackout.

SUNDAY 14TH

Daylight in room.

Clock strikes four.

The door OP opens.

MAN: [*off, at door*] Well, let's keep our fingers crossed. Bye-bye.

MAN *enters, tosses down an overnight bag and a plastic suit carrier.*

He is thoughtful, agitated, pacing nervously. He lights candles on piano, falls dramatically to his knees and makes the sign of the Cross.

Dear God. You know I haven't been to Mass in a long time and that I've done a lot of things that Pope Paul wouldn't approve of. I know I'm in mortal sin and without grace and all that, but listen. I used to be an altar boy and I was a bloody good one, wasn't I? And all those questions on the Assumption and the Resurrection and Transubstantiation, Papal Infallibility, the Trinity, Virgin Birth and all that stuff, I knew it all with footnotes, right? So please, if it's within your power, please don't let it be that Benjamin and Mrs Franklin saw through my drag at the art gallery. Please let them think it was just another fat grannie out with her sister. I know, we both know they were giving us funny looks, but don't let them make the connection, it's extremely important. So please, if they had any suspicion, please dispel it from their minds.

He starts to stand, then kneels again.

And I'll start going to Mass again.

He starts to stand, then kneels again.

Amen.

MAN *makes sign of the Cross.*

Telephone rings.

Shakespeare Speech and Drama. Good … Mrs Franklin!

Blink.

TUESDAY 16TH

Several flashes from camera flashbulb.

Lights up. MAN *is in spot. He takes one final snap.*

MAN: Hmmmmm. Very good, Ben. I should be able to get something from these photos. I don't think it's physical or, um, but well, we'll see. They, er, probably won't be much use but … Okay. Talk to me. What are your other interests besides hairdressers? Have you seen the exhibition at the art gallery? What did you think of it? No, I haven't seen it.

Pause.

Um, do you like sports? Yes, it is pretty boring, isn't it?

Pause.

How's your clap?

Blink.

WEDNESDAY 17TH

Mid-morning.

Telephone rings.

MAN *answers it.*

MAN: Bruce? Hi.

Pause.

I couldn't ring last night. After Ben came, I got smashed. We're in the clear. In fact, Mrs Franklin thinks I'm a genius. She's most effusive about the change I've wrought in Benjamin's speech. How's that, eh? *And* she's got a girlfriend who can't pronounce her W's and she's going to highly recommend me to her. That's the beauty of Double Bay: everyone knows everyone and everyone wants to speak gooder than the next. It's like a big fat rich interwoven network of speech defects.

Pause.

I'm not sure. I think Benjamin knows. It was weird. Like he knew and he knew I knew or knew that I thought he knew or knew I knew he thought it was me—oops—I, but he wasn't going to say anything. As it's our little secret. Anyway, it's alright.

Pause.

Bruce, he wouldn't. I know it. He's a good boy. It doesn't matter. He wouldn't say anything. Look, you're being silly. I don't even know if he knows, so why worry?

Pause.

Look Bruce, I don't give a fuck what the Stock Exchange thinks …

Bruce! What do you want me to do? Shoot him? He doesn't know. Relax. [*Soothing*] Come over now. Right away. Okay? Bye.

MAN *slumps, tired. The sun is setting.*

Telephone rings.

Shakespeare Speech and Drama. Bruce. Don't tell me, let me guess. You're taking Edith and the kids to the circus. You can't come over and you're dreadfully sorry. You wish to offer your apologies, which I accept. You're a creep. Goodbye.

He slams the receiver down.

Telephone rings again immediately.

Listen, shithead—ah, Mrs Franklin? I'm dreadfully sorry, I thought it was someone else. Pardon? … No, um, I don't think so. As far as I'm aware there are no neurotic side effects to speech therapy. He keeps nagging at you to what? To stop going to your hairdresser? Hahaha. Um, no. I can't really explain that, Mrs Franklin. But as a matter of fact, he did tell me that you take him there to get his hair cut. Is that right? Well, he mentioned something about the assistant, the apprentice. I gather she cuts both your hairs, I mean she gives both your heads—ah, pardon? She's a he?

You mean the apprentice is a man?

[*Shocked*] Oh, um. No—I, er, can't explain why he doesn't want you to go there, Mrs, er, Franklin but well, if he's that insistent, perhaps you should change hairdressers. Um, you see, stuttering is a funny sort of thing. No-one can really explain why we stutter. It's a peculiarly Western phenomenon, and, um, he should be under as little pressure as possible. See, there are two schools of thought. If you give in and change hairdressers, you might be spoiling him, thus aggravating his desire for attention, thus prolonging his stutter. Or if you don't back down, then you might be putting more pressure on him and reinforcing his stutter. Do you understand? Look, for the present, Mrs Franklin, take him to a different barber, perhaps a men's barber, and I'll have a chat with him next Tuesday and see what I can find out. Alright? Bye-bye.

MAN *puts down telephone.*

Silence.

He turns to bust.

I'm going to have a serious talk to that boy.

Silence.

He dials on the telephone.

Service-phone? Oh hello, pet. Don't you ever stop working? Listen, take my calls tonight and I'll get them in the morning.

Pause.

Who? Benjamin Franklin? Don't you mean Mrs Franklin? Oh. What was the message? He's what? Would you repeat that? He's got some *better* photos for me? Are you sure that's what he said? Jesus. Um, is that all? Thanks.

MAN *puts down the telephone looks at the bust.*

Jesus, William. The little bastard's trying to seduce me.

Blink.

THURSDAY 18TH

After a long pause:

MAN: [*in spot*] Um. Listen, Benjamin. Did you ring me Wednesday? Uh-huh. You, er, knew it was me, oooops, I, at the art gallery, didn't you? Your mum didn't … thank Christ. Um. And your hairdresser friend who's such a great gobbler is … a man? A boy? Freddy?

Listen Ben, kids of your age often … well, they often … fool around with, um, with kids of their own … sex. It's normal. It's a phase we all go through. But you have to be careful, especially when you do things with older men. Even sixteen-year-old men. Because when you're twelve, well, sixteen is bloody old. Do you understand what I'm saying? I mean that hairdresser could get into all sorts of shit for … interfering with you.

Pause.

Stop preening, Benjamin, this is serious! Listen, I'm flattered that you should want to interfere with me and if you were old enough to know what you were doing then it would be different. I'd probably make like the proverbial rat. But you're not. You're a kid. You're the sort of kid they have on TV to sell Crazy Maze and Kellogg's Cornflakes. You're the sort of kid that judges and juries want to protect from perverts. All the cops have to do is take one look at my rack of dresses and you wouldn't believe the sort of shit they can throw at me. Pederasty, sodomy, corrupting minors, indecent assault on children, homosexual rape, statutory rape.

Pause.

Stop preening! Look, I've been teaching kids long enough to know things have changed. When I was your age, I thought my cock was something you pissed out of then rushed to Confession with at the first sign of tumescence. Huh? Um, stiffening. When I was twelve years old, you see, twelve years old meant twelve years old. It meant you were [*indicating small height*] that tall and you had a bicycle and a dog. I know things are different. Kids are different. It seems like you're all rushing from diapers to dope without stopping to be cute. See. I know. There's something … something weird going on with your generation, like … there's been a nuclear explosion that no-one noticed and we're breeding a race of mutants. But, the point is this. Out there, *Father Knows Best* and *Leave It To Beaver* is the law. If I laid a hand on you, if you told your mum what you know, then I'm fucked. Besides, in spite of that nuclear explosion and the ten-year-old gang-busters and the primary school skinheads and all your big talk and bullshit, you are twelve years old. And I am your teacher. Did you bring those photos?

Let me have them.

He glances at one.

Jesus!

He goes through the rest of them in astonishment.

You ought to be ashamed of yourself. Okay, listen to me. If you've got any more photos, or love-letters, get rid of them. Because, sooner or later, Mum will find them then you're headed for Children's Court—or worse, a psychiatrist—and I'm headed for gaol. Understand? Two. Don't tell *anyone* who's straight what you're doing, because … straights hate. And if anyone talks then we're both in trouble and so's your poxy hairdresser. Three. There is no way that I am going to touch you. I'm too old and I have, believe it or not, a code of ethics. So, you can stop preening like a princess. Four. Think seriously about whether you want to come here. Because if you're not serious about acting, piss off. I can teach you a lot, Benjamin, and I can open doors for you, but it's on my terms. Hmmmm? Five. Try women. I was married to one. They're fun. They've got tits. They feel nice. Try it, you might find you like it.

We hear a car horn outside.

That's your mum.

As we hear front door opening:

And do your bells!

Door closes. Lights slowly come up to reveal room.

Shit! The party!

MAN *hurries off, then re-enters with wig, slip, stuffed bra, high heels. He lights a cigar. He takes his trousers off to reveal pink knickers. He puts on the bra and slip and exits, P.*

He re-enters with dress on.

He starts to put on make-up in front of small mirror. We hear a rock breaking the bay window, loudly.

MAN *looks up, startled.*

The Venetian blinds are open.

Another rock.

VOICE: [*off*] Get out of Double Bay, poofter!
SEVERAL VOICES: Yeah. Get out of here. [*etc., ad lib*]

Another rock.

MAN *closes blinds. Noises continue outside during remainder of scene.*

MAN *walks to telephone, dials.*

MAN: Bruce. It's me. Listen, for once in your life. *Listen*. I want you to take care of Benjamin for me. Take him to David. I haven't got time. There's going to be some nasty things happening. The party's off, pet. Oh … and come visit me, will you? Goodbye.

Another rock comes through the window. MAN *hangs up.*

We hear a police siren.

MAN *makes a pile out of the photos, exits P door, comes back with letters and a notebook, which he shreds into the pile.*

MAN *lights it.*

Knock on door.

VOICE: [*off*] Open up, please. It's the police.

MAN *picks up shotgun.*

MAN: [*sweetly*] Just a minute.
VOICE: [*off*] Alright, you people, shut up and stop throwing those rocks.

Long silence.

Cuckoo clock strikes loudly, MAN *fires at it. It explodes.*

VOICES: [*off*] He's got a gun. Jesus, he fired a gun. [*etc., ad lib*]
VOICE: [*off*] Listen, friend, that won't do you any good.
MAN: [*sweetly*] Just a minute.

MAN *seats himself comfortably with cigar in mouth, watching the pile burn.*

END OF ACT TWO

ACT THREE

Eight years later, a mental hospital.

A bare room with half a dozen beds in a row. There are people in the beds, who hardly move under their covers. MAN *is in centre bed.*

He is 64, looks older. He is subject to long pauses and mispronunciations of words.

The Shakespeare bust is nearby on a table by his bed, its nose broken.

Lights dim to tight spot. From his first speech, MAN *shows absolutely no self-pity.*

MAN: [*to patient in next bed*] McKenzie? You awake? … McKenzie? Nurse! I think McKenzie just died! Yes. [*Cackling*] I think McKenzie died! [*To bust*] William, wipe your nose. I went to a lot of trouble to get you in here. [*Looking around distastefully*] Heh. Don't bother to thank me.

Pause.

Nurse! Someone broke William's nose!

Mumbles of 'Shut up'.

Great bunch of guys in here, William. A laugh a minute. Visiting day tomorrow. That means I get an extra mandy. Yippee. Great invention, Mandrax. Thank Roussel. Do you know, no-one out there can get them now? No sir. They're DAs, William. Drugs of Addiction. Yep. But we get them. Yep. Our government is a pusher, William. McKenzie? Did you fart? You dirty little animal. Jesus, that stinks, doesn't it? William?

He touches bust's nose.

Heh. Heh.

Pause.

Hmmmm? Eleven o'clock? Hmmmm, I suppose that's a.m. Nurse! Nurse! Is it visiting day? Nurse! I want a Mandrax! Nurse, you great fat sow! Hey!

MAN *takes Mandrax from 'nurse'. He swallows it with a glass of water. He watches nurse leave, takes pill out of his mouth, takes a long thin plastic tube out of Shakespeare's ear. It has twenty or thirty pills in it. He places the Mandrax in the tube and puts tube back in bust's ear.*

McKenzie? Is it visiting day today? McKenzie, wake up! Is it visiting day today? McKenzie, wake up! Is it visiting day today? Listen, McKenzie, if you want me to get rid of that Scottish accent for you, you wake up!

Pause.

Are you sure you're not dead? [*Exasperated*] Will someone please tell me whether it's visiting day today?

SEVERAL VOICES: Shut up.

MAN: Is it visiting day today?

SEVERAL VOICES: No!

MAN: Thank you.

Pause.

When is it?

SEVERAL VOICES: Tomorrow! Shut up!

MAN: [*sweetly*] Thanks so much.

Pause.

Visiting day. You know who's coming? Bruce. [*Singing*] 'Sweet Belinda, the peasants call her the goddess of glooooom.' Bruce Fisher the stockbroker is coming to see the Transvestite Terror of Double Bay. You know what I wish? I wish that Bruce could just walk in through that door all dressed up in his Saint Laurent cocktail number, you know [*brushing shoulder*] with those straps and his shoes and his beautiful brown wig and his fucking Gucci handbag and just sit down and be what he fucking wants to be! [*Looking genuinely terrified*] Ooooops. [*To bust*] Might be worth another mandy. Shhhh.

Pause.

Alright, McKenzie, are you ready for your lesson? Hmmmmm? Let's hear you and I don't want [*Scottish accent*] Fred and Frank fought on Friday. Capisce? Come on …McKenzie?

Long bored pause. MAN *grabs clock.*

What time is it? Eleven o'clock. [*To bust*] Alright, William, it's one of three things. It's eleven o'clock tonight. Eleven o'clock the next morning which means it's visiting day, or the same eleven o'clock it was ten minutes ago. Nurse! Which eleven o'clock is it?

Mumbles of 'Shut up'.

If it's eleven o'clock the next day, then it's visiting time and Bruce would be here. If it's eleven o'clock at night, then I would be asleep, because I took a Mandrax … but I didn't take it. There must be a way to tell. Is it dark outside?

MAN *stands up to look through small window above his bed.*

MAN *lies back in bed.*

It's dark. But if it's eleven o'clock at night, why hasn't the nurse told me to shut up? Hmmmm.

MAN *takes thin tube out of bust's ear, takes two pills and lies back.*

Must be night. I'm going to sleep. [*Looking up*] Bruce! My. Don't you look dashing! Oh Christ, don't tell me it's day time. Look, Bruce, pet. In about twenty minutes, I'm going to start raving. But, I don't want you to think it's because I'm—

He taps his head to indicate madness.

I thought it was night time, so I took a couple of mandies, alright? Oh, have you met McKenzie? The Silent But Deadly Kid. McKenzie, Bruce Fisher.

Pause.

How are you? I met your son, the doctor. Jesus, Bruce, isn't he ever going to get rid of those pimples? He had a big yellow one right on the tip of his nose and he: [*Gruffly*] 'Well, Mr O'Brien, and how are we today?' Honest to God, it was all I could do to stop myself from reaching up and busting it. It was huge!

Anyway. I got a cheery note from my lawyer.

'Dear Mr O'Brien. Robert. As expected, the government has denied our petition for release again, using the same old hoary arguments which you may ponder at your leisure.

MAN *looks at enclosed photocopy.*

'We recommend that Robert George O'Brien should not be released from hospital and protective custody. Although homosexuality and transvestism are no longer illegal, nor to be regarded as indications of insanity, the Board finds that the manner of dress and his demeanour at the time of arrest were such as to indicate instability of reason.'

'They're the same ones they used last year and the year before and the year before. But I think we can get you out by next Christmas at the latest and we're going to sue the present government, the previous government, the Mental Health Authority, the Prison's Department, the Hospital, the Commissioner of Police, the Board of Committal, the Attorney General, the Ombudswoman, the Premier and the Crown. In fact, I can't think of anybody in Victoria that we can't sue. Hahaha. Keep your spirits up. We're going to get you out and we're going to get you a million dollars cold. Sincerely, Lindy Stewart.'

She's crazier than I am. Anyway. Oh, and I got this letter from Benjamin.

He takes a letter out of bedside table.

Listen.

[*Reading envelope*] 'St Catherine Hospitel. H-O-S-P-I-T-EL.' E! It's this new education! It's turning out a bunch of morons! Twenty years old and he can't spell.

He examines envelope some more, finds nothing, takes out letter.

'Dear Robert, Finally found a good house in Brunswick.' [*Disgusted*] Brunswick! 'With some very nice poeple …' O-E. 'They were all extremely impressed when I told them that the real live shotgun-totin' Transvestite Terror of Double Bay is a friend of mine. You're quite a celebrity down here too. I've run across half a dozen petitions for your release already. It must have been that *Truth* article the other week that stirred things up. I've decided to go with the National Rock Theatre, Robert. I know you think I should go Old Tote, but that would have meant staying in Sydney with good old Mum and Dad pissing in my pocket. And you know what a pisser she is. Ha. Ha. David is lining up a few other things. They're making a series at Channel Two about the life of Gough Whitlam and it looks like I'll be playing Young Gough from ages sixteen through thirty-five, which would be a real boom boom.' Boom boom? 'But I'll need to have a bigger nose stuck on my own pert little nostrils.' Preen preen. He's always preening. 'I know they examine your mail in that place, hello, Mr Censor, so I've'— [*Turning page*] Hey Nurse! You don't open my mail here, do you? Of course you don't! Benjamin's been reading too many one-handed prison novels. Um, 'so I've sent some photos via a certain lady, if you get my meaning. Haha.' That's you, pet, is it?

Bruce hands him photos.

I'll save them up, I think. 'Oh, I should tell you that I finally took your advice and tried a girl. I didn't like it that much. They're too soft and their tits get in the way. Not as good as the real thing.' [*Looking at Bruce, puzzled*] 'I know you have always forbade me—' Forbade! '—me to involve myself in your case, but, if this appeal fails, I'm going to swear out an affidavit saying that I supplied you with the infamous 'young boy with a banana' photos. They can't hurt me now anyway … it might be good publicity. Haha.' Stupid little bastard! Um. 'I won't be able to get up to Sydney for some time, so take care and don't worry. The government are sure to let you out especially if Labor gets back in, which they will. Because you're on their platform.' How's that, eh? I'm on Labor's platform. The problem is that that makes me not on the Liberals' platform which means that I'll never get out of here. Um … 'Then you can come and live with me in [*sneering*] Brunswick. Keep on fighting, Love, Benjamin.'

Pause. MAN *is moved.*

He drinks water, picks up photos and goes through them. He puts them under the bust.

My. Don't you look dashing, Bruce? I, er, I, er, I had a bet with William that you'd come in drag. But, er, I, er—see? Heh. [*Cackling*] I, er, don't know much about crazy people even, er, even though I've been around them so long. But … What I've always thought was, er, that a crazy man couldn't say he was crazy. He could never say it. It might be a lot of bullshit. But, er, that's what I've always believed. So every morning, when I wake up, I say: 'I'm as crazy as a snake.' Like that see? 'I'm as crazy as a snake.' Then I know that I'm not. Like. But this morning, I had to force myself to say it. It was hard, Bruce. I thought: 'Well, why bother? Don't say it this morning, don't worry about it, say it tomorrow.' But see, I knew that if, er, if the morning ever came when I couldn't say I was, er, I was, er, crazy then I would be. Do you understand? I would be if I couldn't say I was. I, er, don't want to be crazy, Bruce. I like my mind. I don't want it to go. I, er, see, the only reason I was able to stand it, the trial and the publicity and the … was that, er, when a judge or a reporter said, 'You're mad,' I'd say, 'That's right, I'm as crazy as a snake,' and … do you know? Do you know? I … I'm a Catholic, Bruce. I've always believed that if you didn't have a mind then you didn't have a soul either and if you didn't have a soul then you, er, then you wouldn't even make it to hell. You'd er, just stop.

Pause.

I don't want to stop. See, I don't give a shit if I go to heaven or hell or purgatory or limbo or what but I want to go somewhere. I don't want to stop. Do you know? Do you know? Father Thompson, he says that, er, that crazy people have, um, angels in them. That God loves them so much he sends them a bit of heaven and that's where their minds are. But, er, that's not true. That's not true. I've seen the crazy ones and they're not in heaven. They've lost their souls, Bruce. They've lost their souls. See, I've been a bad, er, man and my soul is black but I've still, er, got one. But I *don't want to lose my soul*!

Blink.

MAN *awakes.*

I'm as crazy as a snake. [*Grinning, then sweetly*] Nurse. Oh, nurse? Why don't you take the straps off? Nurse? What's the matter? Haven't you ever lost your temper? You big fat bitch! Take off these straps! [*Looking at bed next to him*] Stop looking at me like that, McKenzie! I'm alright! Stop looking at me, like I'm crazy!

Come on, Nurse! Take the fucking things off! Please! That's the problem, William, you fly off the handle once, then you can't convince anyone that you're not waiting to get your hands around their throats. I'm warning you, [*to next bed*] I've seen you when you were Genghis Khan's brother but I'm always nice to you, you prick. Nurse? Would you call Doctor Savage? Please? I'll do poos in my bed. Thank you. [*To bust*] She's a nice lady. [*To McKenzie*] As for you, shitface, if you ever show your farting arsehole around here trying to get free speech lessons, I *will* strangle you.

Pause.

Stop crying, McKenzie, I'm only joking.

Silence.

MAN *struggles with straps.*

Doctor? I'm alright now, thank you. Will you please take these …

He lifts his hands up, showing that there are no straps.

…straps … Heh. [*Cackling*] April fool. [*Watching doctor leave*] Yep. April fool.

MAN *tries straps again, puzzled.*

He puts his arms around bust for comfort, very sad and worried.

FIRST VOICE: [*disc jockey, on radio*] This is Two RB. And you're with Talkback …

Music.

Two RB, the friendly station … yeah. Today we're talking about the Transvestite Terror of Double Bay. We'd like to hear your views so ring us on two oh six two five seven. Now.

Commercial for Coca Cola.

Hello?

SECOND VOICE: [*male, on telephone*] Hello? Is that Talkback?

FIRST VOICE: Yes.

SECOND VOICE: My name is Stuart Coffen, I'm on the Committee for the Release of Sexual-Political Prisoners and we have currently over forty thousand signatures on our release petition. It is our belief that—

FIRST VOICE: Can you make it brief please, Stuart, we have a lot of callers on the line.

SECOND VOICE: Certainly. Briefly the CRSPP believes that Robert O'Brien is a harmless old man who has been denied his rights under Section Nine of the Australian Bill of Rights in that he has been subject to imprisonment without trial—

FIRST VOICE: But he had a trial.

SECOND VOICE: No. He only appeared before a Committal Board but—

FIRST VOICE: Thanks for your call, Stuart, we—

SECOND VOICE: What the—

Beep.

—is everyone so afraid of? No-one wants to discuss this case in a rational and detailed manner.

Cut off.

FIRST VOICE: Please remember your language, Stuart. In case you've forgotten, it was the management of Two RB that elected to discuss this man in the public interest. Hello?

THIRD VOICE: [*female, on telephone*] Hello? Talkback?

FIRST VOICE: Yes. Go ahead.

THIRD VOICE: I'm a mother.

Silence.

FIRST VOICE: Yes?

THIRD VOICE: I'm a mother. I have three children. One is a little boy the same age as that—

Beep beep.

—at the—

FIRST VOICE: Madam, we're not allowed to name the child.

THIRD VOICE: But his name was in the paper.

FIRST VOICE: Yes, but—could you please say what you have to say?

THIRD VOICE: Yes. I'm a mother. I have three children. One is a little boy the same age as—

Beep beep.

—lin at the time of the shootout. I think animals like this should be kept locked away forever for their own good as much as society's.

I mean, how would you like it if your son was forced to pose for pornographic photos for some pervert like Robert O'Brien. No. I reckon the government's doing the right thing in keeping him locked up.

FIRST VOICE: Well, thank you, Madam. We'll be back with the Transvestite Terror of Double Bay in just a moment.

Ad for Myer's. Ad for pimple cream.

You're on Talkback with … Two RB the friendly station … yeah. Go ahead.

FOURTH VOICE: [*male, on telephone*] My name is George. I took speech lessons from Robert O'Brien for a couple of weeks before I realised what sort of man he was.

FIRST VOICE: What sort of man was that?

FOURTH VOICE: A homo … homosens …

FIRST VOICE: Homosexual?

FOURTH VOICE: Yes. I stopped going when I realised that.

FIRST VOICE: Did he make a pass at you?

FOURTH VOICE: How do you mean?

FIRST VOICE: Well, how did you know he was homosexual?

FOURTH VOICE: Oh. Well, you know. You can tell. He acted funny. He used to call me pet.

FIRST VOICE: Pet?

FOURTH VOICE: Pet.

Pause.

FIRST VOICE: Is there anything else you can tell us about him?

FOURTH VOICE: Yes. He molested young children.

FIRST VOICE: He hasn't been accused of molesting children.

FOURTH VOICE: What about those photos of Ben—

Beep beep.

FIRST VOICE: Yes. Well. Thanks for your call.

FIRST VOICE: Hello?

FIFTH VOICE: [*male, on telephone*] Yeah. you're not trying to tell me that creep was interested in the elocution of that boy with the bananas?

FIRST VOICE: I'm not trying to tell you anything.

FIFTH VOICE: Yeah. Good. Don't tell me he was trying to teach these kids to speak. He just wanted to … to … well, you know.

FIRST VOICE: Thanks for your opinion.

FIFTH VOICE: Yeah.

FIRST VOICE: Hello?

Pause.

Hello?

MAN: [*his voice on telephone*] Do you think a man loses his soul when he goes mad?

FIRST VOICE: Hello?

MAN: [*on telephone*] Do you think it's better for a man to go to hell than just to stop?

FIRST VOICE: Sir. We're talking about the Transvestite Terror of Double Bay. Do you have something to say on that subject?

MAN: [*on telephone*] Yes.

FIRST VOICE: Yes?

Pause.

Do you have something to say about him?

MAN: Help me.

FIRST VOICE: Pardon?

MAN: Help me.

Ad for Coca Cola.

Sound fades down.

MAN *is in bed. The other beds are dimly discerned. They begin to roll away one by one.* MAN *is left alone.*

He reaches under bust and takes out the photos.

He looks at them.

Oh, Ben.

MAN *picks up the long thin tube. It is empty. He places it in bust's ear, pats bust affectionately.*

He looks at the photos of Ben some more.

THE END

GRIFFIN THEATRE COMPANY PRESENTS

THE ELOCUTION OF BENJAMIN FRANKLIN

BY steve j. spears

21 FEB – 29 MAR 2026

DOWNSTAIRS THEATRE, BELVOIR ST THEATRE

GRIFFIN
THEATRE
COMPANY

CAST & CREATIVES

Director Declan Greene
Designer Isabel Hudson
Lighting Designer BROCKMAN
Composer & Sound Designer David Bergman
Community Engagement Strategist Bayley Turner
Vocal Coach Linda Nicholls-Gidley
Intimacy Coordinator Chloë Dallimore
Producer Gus Murray
Stage Manager Isabella Kerdijk
With Simon Burke AO

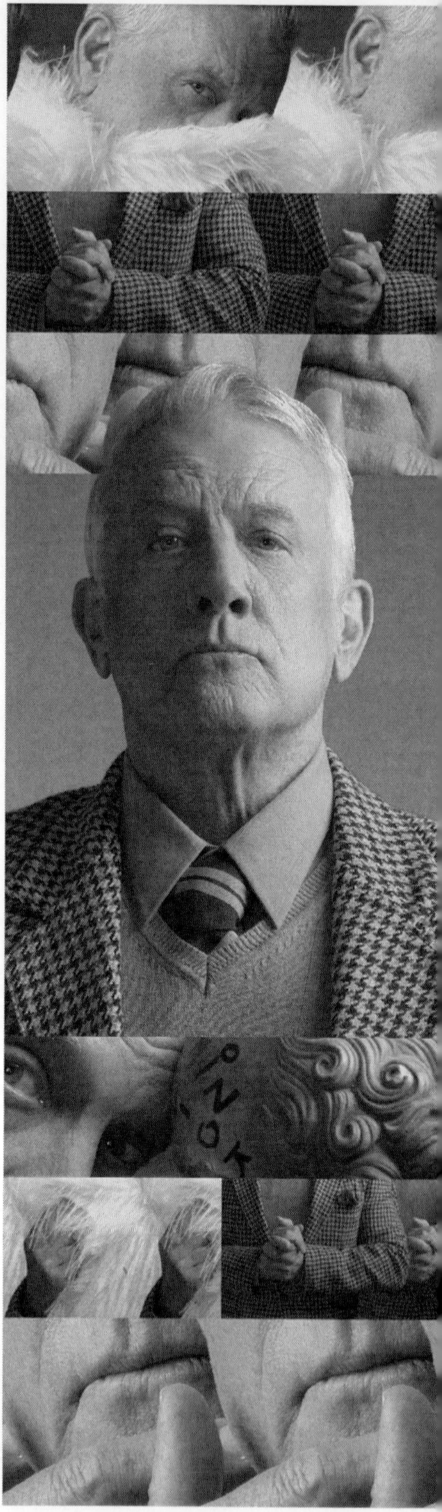

SUPPORTED BY

SALLY BREEN
FAMILY FOUNDATION

GOVERNMENT PARTNERS

Creative Australia

NSW GOVERNMENT

The Elocution of Benjamin Franklin is made possible with the support of the Sally Breen Family Foundation and the Griffin Redraft Fund.

DIRECTOR'S NOTE

"The greater the number of homosexuals the greater the threat to innocent boys."

Sir Peter Delamothe OBE (Attorney-General of Queensland 1963–71)

In 1976, **steve j. spears** premiered a play about a gay man who is destroyed by a very old moral hysteria. The idea that queer people are, somehow, inherently dangerous to children.

The Elocution of Benjamin Franklin is a portrait of a time. In Australia: **David Bowie, The Skyhooks,** *The Rocky Horror Picture Show,* **Betty Blokkbuster** were all wildly popular entertainment. In 1976, male flamboyance, it seemed, was passable. But if that flamboyance was conflated with *homosexuality*, it was not. Male homosexual activity remained illegal in every Australian state except the ACT and South Australia. As retort to the growing push for decriminalisation, one idea was parroted endlessly on the nightly news, by men like **Peter Delamonthe**: *gay men will harm your children*. Then, change the channel—there's **Red Symonds** on *Countdown* playing guitar in a feather boa and lipstick, as **Shirley Strachan** sings *"I feel a little mixed up / I feel a little queer..."*—to screaming crowds of teenage boys and girls.

In *The Elocution of Benjamin Franklin*, steve j. spears's towering anti-hero Robert O'Brien does not harm his voice students. Yet, when his sexuality is exposed, it becomes a pretext for accusation, incarceration and worse. With all the play's shock value (including its infamous nude opening), it can be easy overlook how radical it was for spears to write, at that time, a play about a homosexual teacher of children. And one who was—in the words of **Richard Wherett AM**—a *"fiercely honourable and principled"* man, but *"trapped by the hypocritically puritanical society of the 1970s."*

***

Six years ago I sent this play to **Simon Burke**, feeling in my gut that—should I ever get to direct *The Elocution of Benjamin Franklin*—he was the person to take on this role. And so we circled this work for years: tantalised, terrified and waiting for the moment when a revival felt not only necessary, but urgent.

That urgency did not arrive in a single flash. It came as a slow accumulation. A tumble of troubling occurrences that eventually built into a landslide. Last year, Liberal senator **Alex Antic** asked the ABC why they were "grooming children" by allowing a gay man in a dress—**Courtney Act**—to read a picture book on *Play School*. Hysteria reignited around the rights of trans women to access bathrooms. Sex education for queer students was banned in schools across the United States—which might feel distant, until we remember that our own moral panic around the Safe Schools program was only seven years ago.

It is both uncanny and tragic that *The Elocution of Benjamin Franklin* is now fifty years old and yet it understands this contemporary hysteria intimately.

To make that resonance as clear as possible in this production, I am grateful to the estate of steve j. spears for trusting us to adapt aspects of the play—including returning its location to Double Bay, as in its original staging, rather than the later relocation to Toorak.

***

This is not to say, of course, that *The Elocution of Benjamin Franklin* is a morally perfect vessel for this message.

DIRECTOR'S NOTE

It would be boring if it was. Like its protagonist, *The Elocution of Benjamin Franklin* is larger-then-life, grotesque, contradictory and uses humour in a way that is discombobulating, especially for some contemporary sensibilities.

It still astounds me that when *The Elocution of Benjamin Franklin* was first produced, it was received largely as a raucous comedy. Its iconic original star **Gordon Chater AM**, beloved from *The Mavis Bramston Show*, drew in audiences ready to laugh—and they did.

A great deal has changed since 1976. The Catholic church scandals of the 90s fundamentally reshaped our cultural understanding of child abuse. spears dared us to laugh at the absurd transgression of a child attempting to seduce his revolting, ridiculous sissy of teacher. Yet in 2026 this idea carries a gravity that resists comedy, irony, or theatrical play.

As I write this, deep in rehearsals, Simon and I can feel that resonance of this story. Its tragedy, its triumph, its emotional heft—its *"diatribe about injustice"*, to quote Chater. But we genuinely do not know how funny audiences will find it anymore. *The Elocution of Benjamin Franklin* dares us to laugh—with the blackest humour—at the machinery of accusation, at hysteria itself. But it also brushes uncomfortably close to material we now refuse to treat lightly. I daresay this is part of the reason why the play has not been produced, professionally, in 24 years.

With this production, we are attempting to live inside that tension. Inside spears's righteous anger and the rough, troubling, majestic play he forged to contain it. I am deeply grateful to all who have assisted us on the preparation of this production—in particular **Anthony Blair, Rob George, Bayley Turner**—as well as my colleagues at Griffin, for their careful and patient stewardship of this idea over many years. And above all, I am grateful to Simon.

Declan Greene
Director

PERFORMER'S NOTE

"See, I think all he needs is a father figure" [sipping daintily]

Robert O'Brien in *The Elocution of Benjamin Franklin*

One afternoon in 1974, my somewhat unfatherly father picked me up from school and drove me to the new Nimrod Theatre (now Belvoir St Theatre) for my first ever audition—a new Australian play that **Richard Wherrett AM** was directing. I was 12 years old (the same age as Benjamin Franklin is in our play). Richard led me to the Upstairs Theatre, handed me a page of script and told me to go down to the stage and sight read it for him. The kid in the play had to swear like a trooper and he obviously wanted to see if I was spooked by "language". I was not. I settled myself, took a deep breath and let rip, my little alto tones spraying the back of the house with the foulest language I'd never dared voice. I can still see the look on Richard's face; a little shocked, kind of delighted, and clearly trying to suppress a giggle. I got the part, did the play and I've been doing plays ever since.

Richard and I only worked together a couple more times over the years but from that day until his death in 2001 he was a towering figure in my life. Warm and distant, imperious and impetuous, stern and indulgent, ribald and censorious, high and low (low, low) brow, always ready with the best—and the worst—advice, a perfect gentleman and camp as fuck. I loved him with all my heart. Rehearsing this play I find myself freshly grateful to Richard and the other unconventional father figures that I encountered as a young adult, whose wholly safe and positive influences on me sprang from a mutual recognition of sameness in a world that spurned difference.

To be back in this building where it all began for me, to essay this monumentally challenging role in this unexploded landmine of a play in the same theatre that Richard first directed it exactly 50 years ago feels like almost unbearably sweet serendipity. And for that I thank **Declan**, for whom and with whom I would do anything. Onstage that is.

Simon Burke AO
Performer

BIOGRAPHIES

steve j. spears

PLAYWRIGHT

Steve's theatre credits included: for Griffin Theatre Company: *Glory, When They Send Me Three and Fourpence*; for Actors Co of Cleveland: *Froggie*, which received the Cleveland Critics Circle Award; for Circle Theatre: *People Keep Giving Me Things*; for Crossroads: *Namatjira Park*; for La Boite Theatre: *King Richard*, which he later adapted for radio and won the AWGIE; for Pram Factory: *Africa*; for Nimrod Theatre: *The Elocution of Benjamin Franklin* went on to become an international success, touring three continents and winning the OBIE for Best Play Off-Broadway and AWGIE for Best Play, *There Were Giants in Those Days* and *Young Mo*, which earned the National Critics' Circle Awards for Best New Talent and Best Play; for Stage Company: *The Death of George Reeves, Those Dear Departed*; and for State Youth Theatre: *Mad Jean*.

Steve's television credits included: for the Australian Children's Television Foundation: *The Greatest Tune on Earth*, winning the Penguin Certificate of Merit; for Network Ten: *E Street, Heartbreak High, Winners*, nominated for AFI's Best Children's Drama and Best Screenplay and winning Chicago's International Festival of Children's Films Award for Outstanding Humour; for Nine Network: *All Together Now, Chances*; and for Seven Network: *A Country Practice, Hey Dad!, Sky Trackers*.

Steve died in 2007.

BIOGRAPHIES

DECLAN GREENE

DIRECTOR

Declan Greene is Artistic Director of Griffin Theatre Company.

Declan's credits as a director include: for Griffin Theatre Company: *Dogged*, *Green Park*, *Naturism, Sex Magick* (co-directed with Nicholas Brown), *The Lewis Trilogy*, *Whitefella Yella Tree* (co-directed with Amy Sole); Sydney Theatre Company: *Hamlet*, *Prince of Skidmark*; Griffin Theatre Company and Hayes Theatre Co: *Flat Earthers: The Musical*; Malthouse Theatre: *Wake in Fright*; for Malthouse Theatre and Sydney Theatre Company: *Blackie Blackie Brown*; ZLMD Shakespeare Company: *Conviction*. As a playwright: *Eight Gigabytes of Hardcore Pornography*, *The Homosexuals, or 'Faggots'*, *Melancholia*, *Pompeii L.A.* and *Moth*.

Declan co-founded queer experimental theatre company Sisters Grimm with Ash Flanders in 2006, and has directed and co-created all their productions to date, including: for Griffin Independent and Theatre Works: *Summertime in the Garden of Eden*; for Malthouse Theatre and Sydney Theatre Company: *Calpurnia Descending*; for Melbourne Theatre Company: *Lilith: The Jungle Girl*; and for Sydney Theatre Company: *Little Mercy*. He was previously Resident Artist at Malthouse Theatre.

ISABEL HUDSON

DESIGNER

Isabel is an award-winning set and costume designer. Isabel's design credits for the stage include: for Griffin Theatre Company: *Ghosting the Party, Jailbaby, Pony, Nucleus*; for Belvoir St Theatre: *Blessed Union, Every Brilliant Thing, Winyanboga Yurringa*; for Belvoir 25A: *Jess & Joe Forever, Tuesday;* for Ensemble Theatre: *Master Class*; for Hayes Theatre Co: *American Psycho, Cry-Baby, Young Frankenstein, Razorhurst, The View Upstairs*; for Melbourne Theatre Company: *Torch the Place*; for New Theatricals: *Darkness*; for NIDA: *Mr Burns*; for Pinchgut Opera: *Farnace*; for Shake and Stir: *The Lovers*; for Sydney Festival/Rising/Darwin Festival: *Maureen: Harbinger of Death*; for Sydney Theatre Company: *A Fool In Love, Constellations, Hubris & Humiliation.* Isabel was the costume designer for *Dear Evan Hansen* (Michael Cassel Group) and costume designer and associate set designer for *The Mousetrap* (Crossroads Productions). Isabel has won four Sydney Theatre Awards for her outstanding designs; best set design for *Constellations, American Psycho*, and *Cry-Baby,* and best costume design for *Hubris And Humiliation*. She also won an APDG award for best set design for *American Psycho*. She was awarded the Kristian Fredrikson Scholarship in 2022 and The Thelma Afford Award for Costume Design in Stage and Screen in 2022

BIOGRAPHIES

BROCKMAN

LIGHTING DESIGNER

BROCKMAN is an award-winning lighting and set designer who has worked both in Australia and internationally.

For Griffin Theatre Company: *Diving For Pearls, Family Values, Replay, Splinter;* for Griffin Theatre Company and Hayes Theatre Co: *Flat Earthers: The Musical*; for bAKEHOUSE: *Coram Boy, Dresden, Visiting Hours, The Laden Table, Jatinga*; for Belvoir 25a: *Horses, Jess & Joe Forever, Greater Sunrise*; for Campbelltown Arts Centre: *Mirage, Apocalypse, Cleansed, Metamorphoses, Angels In America Part 1 And 2*; for CDP: *Are we there yet?, Guess How Much I Love You, Spot Live On Stage*; for Critical Stages: *Alphabetical Sydney*; for Dance Makers Collective: *The Rivoli, Wolverine*; for Darlinghurst Theatre Company: *Overflow, Torch Song Trilogy, Broken, Detroit, Mother Fucker With A Hat, Tinder Box*; for Ensemble Theatre Company: *Tribes, The Big Dry, The Plant, Neville's Island*; for Hayes Theatre Co: *Ride The Cyclone, Gentlemen Prefer Blondes, Carmen Alive Or Dead, Razorhurst*; for Legs On The Wall: *Cat's Cradle, The Raft, Waters Edge*; for Little Eggs Collective: *Symphonie Fantastique*; for National Theatre Of Paramatta: *Things Hidden Since The Foundation Of The World (AUS/UK), Lady Tabouli, Girl In The Machine, The Girl/ The Woman, The Sorry Mum Project, Let Me Know When You Get Home*; Pinchgut Opera: *Farnace*; for Queensland Theatre Company: *Family Values*; for Shaun Parker & Company: *In The Zone, King*; for Squabbalogic: *Day of the triffids development, Good Omens The Musical development, Herringbone, Grey Gardens The Musical, Man Of La Mancha*; Sydney Mardi Gras Festival: *Sissy Ball 2022, Sissy Ball 2020*; Sydney Theatre Company: *Constellations, A Fool In Love, American Signs.*

BIOGRAPHIES

DAVID BERGMAN

COMPOSER & SOUND DESIGNER

David's designs for theatre include: for Griffin Theatre Company: sound designer *Green Park*, composer and sound designer *Superheroes*, composer, sound and video designer *First Love Is The Revolution*, composer and sound designer, *Naturism;* for Bell Shakespeare: sound designer *Twelfth Night, The Lovers*: for Belvoir St Theatre: composer and sound designer *Scenes From The Climate Era*, sound designer *Into The Woods*, video designer *Blue*, sound designer *At What Cost?*; for Ensemble Theatre: composer and sound designer *Aria, Memory Of Water*; for Hayes Theatre Co: sound and video designer *Merrily We Roll Along*, sound designer *Dubbo Championship Wrestling, The Rise And Disguise Of Elizabeth R., Catch Me If You Can, Spring Awakening*; for Michael Cassel Group: video design *Dear Evan Hansen*; for Monkey Baa Theatre; video designer *Possum Magic, The Peasant Prince*, sound designer *Josephine Wants To Dance*; for Shake and Stir: *The Lovers*; for Soft Tread: video and sound design T*he Gospel According To Paul*; for Sydney Theatre Company: video designer *The Picture of Dorian Gray, Strange Case of Dr Jekyll and Mr Hyde*, sound design *Playing Beatie Bow*, video and sound design *A Cheery Soul and The Wharf Revue* (from 2009-2018), video design *Julius Caesar, Muriel's Wedding: The Musical, The Hanging, The Effect, The Long Way Home.* David has won two Sydney Theatre Company awards: for Best Stage Design of a Mainstage Production for *The Picture of Dorian Gray* and for Best Sound Design of a Mainstage Production for *Green Park*.

BIOGRAPHIES

BAYLEY TURNER

COMMUNITY ENGAGEMENT STRATEGIST

Bayley Turner (she/her) is a consultant on consent-based practice, inclusion, and intimacy coordination. As Consent and Intimacy Consultant: for Griffin Theatre Company: *Jailbaby, The Lewis Trilogy, swim;* for Griffin Theatre Company and Sydney Theatre Company: *Whitefella Yella Tree*; for Andrew Henry Presents: *Hedwig and the Angry Inch*; for Bullet Heart Club: *The Hall, In The Club, The Inheritance, The Placeholder, Things I Know to Be True*; for Malthouse Theatre: *Truth*; for Melbourne Theatre Company: *The Almighty Sometimes*; for Michael Cassel Group: *Hamilton;* for Sydney Theatre Company: *Sweat*; for Victorian College of the Arts: *Spring Awakening*; for Bunya Productions: *Ladies in Black*; Fremantle Media: *Neighbours*; and as Performer: for Black Apple Theatre: *Thrive: Queer Voices Out Loud*; for Bullet Heart Club and fortyfive downstairs: *Thirty-Six*; for Mean Projects: *Burlesque by Force*. Bayley has trained with Intimacy On Set and IDC Professionals. Bayley has also presented at various conferences and events on consent in the creative sector, including Creative Toolkit 2024, and SXSW 2024, 2025. Bayley is honoured to be part of trans storytelling and truth-telling working with the next generation of artists. @createconsent

BIOGRAPHIES

LINDA NICHOLLS-GIDLEY

VOCAL COACH

Linda's theatre credits include: for Griffin Theatre Company: *Pony*; for Crossroads Live: *Cluedo, Back to the Future, Annie, The Odd Couple, Cinderella, 9 to 5, An American in Paris*; for Darlinghurst Theatre Company: *Let the Right One In, Once, A Chorus Line, I'm With Her, The Rise and Fall of Little Voice, Love; for Dreamworks: How To Train Your Dragon – Arena Spectacular*; for Ensemble Theatre: *True West, Primary Trust, The Half-Life of Marie Curie, The Lover/The Dumb Waiter, The Glass Menagerie, The Heartbreak Choir, Colder Than Here, Master Class, Ulster American, Switzerland, Alone it Stands, The Memory of Water, Summer of Harold, Benefactors, Clyde's, Suddenly Last Summer, Boxing Day BBQ, The Caretaker, Photograph 51, Black Cockatoo, Baby Doll, The Last Five Years; for Gordon Frost: The Rocky Horror Show, Shrek, Saturday Night Fever, The Bodyguard, Dirty Dancing*; for GWB Entertainment: T*he Lord of The Rings – A Musical Tale, Hedwig and the Angry Inch, Jagged Little Pill, Girl From the North Country, An American in Paris*; for Hayes Theatre Co: *Ride The Cyclone, Zombie!, Murder for Two, Jekyll and Hyde*; for Jones Theatricals: *Pretty Woman;* for Matt Ward Productions: *Beautiful*; for Monkey Baa Theatre: *Hitler's Daughter*; for NTofP: *Daytime Deewane, Yoga Play, Fade, Grounded*; for New Theatricals: *Gaslight*; for Opera Australia: *Guys and Dolls, Miss Saigon*; for Outhouse Theatre: *Eureka Day, A Case for the Existence of God, Consent, Heroes of the Fourth Turning*; for Playlab: *Slow Boat*; for TEG Dainty: *Tina*; for Seymour Centre: *The Inheritance, Museum of Modern Love*; for Sport For Jove: *Betrayal, The Player Kings, Isolde and Tristan, The Crucible*.

Linda's television credits include: for Paramount +: *Shantaram*; for Netflix: *Wellmania*; for Stan: *Year Of*; for Fremantle: *Mary: The Making of a Princess.*

Lindas' film credits include *We Will Never Die, Sleeping Dogs, Seeds of Gold, Jungle.*

BIOGRAPHIES

CHLOË DALLIMORE

INTIMACY COORDINATOR

Chloë is an internationally trained and accredited Intimacy Coordinator/Director. Theatre: for Griffin Theatre Company: *Blaque Showgirls, Naturism, Sex Magick*; for Griffin Theatre Company and Hayes Theatre Co: *Flat Earthers: The Musical*; for Belvoir St Theatre: *At What Cost?, Big Girls Don't Cry, Miss Peony, The Master & Margarita*; for Crossroads Live: *Chicago, The Rocky Horror Show, Wicked*; for Hayes Theatre Co: *Jekyll and Hyde, The Pirates of Penzance, Ride The Cyclone, Zombie!*; for Opera Australia: *Amadeus, Hadestown, Miss Saigon, RENT, Summer Season '26*; for Sydney Theatre Company: *Circle Mirror Transformation, Dear Evan Hansen, The Importance of Being Earnest, The Shiralee, The Talented Mr Ripley.*

Film: for Stan: *Bump Christmas (2025)*; for Columbia Pictures, *Screen Gems*, and Original Film: *I Know What You Did Last Summer (2025)*; for Amazon MGM Studios: *Play Dirty (2025)*; for Raimi Productions, 20th Century Studios and TSG Entertainment: *Send Help (2026)*.

Television: for Binge: *Mix Tape, Strife, The Last Anniversary, The Twelve*; for Netflix: *Heartbreak High, Wellmania*; for Paramount+: *Last King of the Cross, NCIS: Sydney, Playing Gracie Darling*; for Stan: *Bump, Colin From Accounts, Last King of the Cross.*

Chloë received the Australian Entertainment Mo Award for Female Musical Theatre Performer (2004), the Helpmann Award for Best Female Actor in a Musical (2005), the Sydney Theatre Award for Best Actress in a Supporting Role (2005), the Victorian Green Room Association Awards for Best Leading Female Artist in Music Theatre (2005).

ISABELLA KERDIJK

STAGE MANAGER

Isabella graduated from the production course at the National Institute of Dramatic Art in 2008. She has worked as a Stage Manager and Assistant Stage Manager on many shows, including: for Griffin Theatre Company: *And No More Shall We Part, Blaque Showgirls, Green Park, Replay, Sex Magick, swim, The Smallest Hour, This Year's Ashes, Ugly Mugs, Whitefella Yella Tree, Wicked Sisters*; for Belvoir St Theatre: *Big Girls Don't Cry, An Enemy of the People, The Dog/The Cat, The Drover's Wife, Every Brilliant Thing, FANGIRLS, Girl Asleep, The Glass Menagerie, HIR, Jasper Jones, Kill the Messenger, Mother, Mother Courage and Her Children, My Name is Jimi, Stories I Want to Tell You In Person, The Sugar House, Thyestes (European Tours), Well-Behaved Women, Winyanboga Yurringa*; for Sydney Theatre Company; *Blithe Spirit*; for Circus Oz: *Cranked Up*; for Darlinghurst Theatre Company: *Fourplay, Ride, Silent Night*; for Ensemble Theatre: *Benefactors, Boxing Day BBQ, Rainman, The Half-Life of Marie Curie, The Ruby Sunrise; for Legs on the Wall: Bubble*; for LWAA: *The Mousetrap* (Australia/New Zealand Tours); for Spiegelworld: *Empire*; for Sydney Festival: *A Model Murder.*

BIOGRAPHIES

SIMON BURKE AO

ROBERT O'BRIEN

In 2015, Simon was named an Officer of the Order of Australia (AO) *"for distinguished service to the performing arts as an actor, singer and producer"*.

Australian stage credits include for Griffin Theatre Company: *The Homosexuals, October, Satango*; for Sydney Theatre Company: *Mary Stuart, Mrs Warren's Profession and The Wharf Revue* (2013, 2017 & 2019); for Griffin Theatre Company and Bell Shakespeare: *The Misanthrope*; for Melbourne Theatre Company: *Noises Off, Three Furies* (Sydney/Auckland/Perth/Adelaide Festivals); for Seymour Centre: *Strangers In Between*. He starred in *The Inheritance* (2025 Sydney Theatre Award for Best Ensemble and Best Independent Production).

Australian musical theatre credits include: *Wicked* (The Wizard) the Australasian tour; *Moulin Rouge! The Musical* (Harold Zidler, for which he won a Sydney Theatre Award for Best Performance in a Supporting Role-Musical); *Catch Me If You Can* (Frank Abignale); *Hairspray* (Edna); *Clinton The Musical* (Bill Clinton); *Mary Poppins* (Mr Banks); *Chicago* (Billy Flynn); *Anything Goes* (Billy Crocker, for which he won a Green Room Award Best Actor – Musical), *Les Miserables* (as Marius in the original Australian cast).

London West End credits include: *The Sound of Music* (Captain von Trapp); *The Phantom of the Opera* (Raoul); *A Little Night Music* (Carl-Magnus); *La Cage Aux Folles*(Georges); UK premiere of *Holding the Man; When The Rain Stops Falling* (Almeida Theatre).

Film and Television credits include: *The Devil's Playground* (1976 AFI Best Actor Award), *Devil's Playground* (Executive Producer, 2015 AACTA and Logie Award for Best Mini-Series), 25 years presenting *Play School* and the upcoming *Five Minute Call* (producer and co-writer).

Federal President of Actors Equity for MEAA 2004-2014, Vice President of FIA (International Federation of Actors) 2012-2016. Awarded Actors Equity Life Membership Award in 2015.

ABOUT GRIFFIN

Griffin is the only theatre company in the country exclusively devoted to the development and staging of new Australian writing. Located in the historic SBW Stables Theatre, nestled in the heart of Kings Cross, Griffin has been Australia's home for the exploration of new stories since 1979.

We are the launch pad for new plays, ideas and writing that other theatres won't take a risk on. We boldly contribute to Australia's unique and powerful storytelling culture. Plays like *Prima Facie*, *Holding the Man* and *City of Gold* all had their world premieres at Griffin before going out to capture the national imagination. In the words of our longest-serving Artistic Director, **Ros Horin**:

"We are the theatre of first chances."

We are passionate about nurturing emerging and established practitioners alike. We pride ourselves on supporting our vast community of artists, audiences and supporters who consider our theatre their creative home. We help ambitious, bold, risk-taking and urgent Australian work get from the page onto the stage. We tell the stories that help us know who we are as a nation and who we want to become.

Acknowledgement of Country

Griffin Theatre Company operates and tells stories on the unceded lands of the Gadigal of the Eora Nation. We acknowledge and honour Aboriginal and Torres Strait Islander people as the oldest continuous living culture on the planet, with more than 60,000 years of storytelling practice shaping and underpinning all aspects of Australian culture. It is a privilege that we do not take lightly: to work on this land, and to tell stories on its soil.

GRIFFIN THEATRE COMPANY
13 Craigend St
Gadigal Land, Kings Cross, NSW 2011

CONTACT
02 9332 1052
info@griffintheatre.com.au
griffintheatre.com.au

GRIFFIN FAMILY

Board
Bruce Meagher (Chair)
Guillaume Babille
Nigel Barrington
Simon Burke AO
Julieanne Campbell
Jane Clifford
Declan Greene
Julia Pincus
Lenore Robertson AM
Simone Whetton

Artistic Director and Co-CEO
Declan Greene

Executive Director and Co-CEO
Julieanne Campbell

General Manager
Khym Scott

Associate Artistic Director
Anthea Williams

Literary Associate
Daley Rangi

Associate Producer
Cassie Hamilton

Head of Development
Jake Shavikin

Relationship Manager
Harry Lyddiard

Marketing Manager
Erica Penollar

Marketing and Content Producer
Christie Yip

Ticketing Manager
Gavin Roach

Ticketing Administrator
Nathan Harrison

Front of House Manager
Alex Bryant-Smith

Front of House
Riordan Berry,
Max Philips,
Maddy Withington

Administrator
Blake Hahn

Production Manager
Jimi Rawlings

Production and Technical Coordinator
Amy Norton

Finance Manager
Chrissy Riley

Finance Consultant
Emma Murphy

Publicity
Kabuku PR

Graphic Design
Susu Studio

Cover Photography
Daniel Boud

Web Developer
DevQuoll

ABOUT BELVOIR ST THEATRE

Belvoir St Theatre is a theatre company on a side street in Surry Hills, Sydney.

We share our street with a park and a public housing estate, and our theatre is in an old industrial building. It has been, at various times, a garage, a sauce factory, and the Nimrod Theatre. When the theatre was threatened with redevelopment in 1984, over 600 likeminded theatre-lovers formed a syndicate to buy the building and save it from becoming an apartment block. More than thirty years later, Belvoir continues to be at the forefront of Australian acting and storytelling for the stage. In 2026, that story takes a new turn. While Griffin Theatre Company's home is being redeveloped, Belvoir's Downstairs will be its temporary base. Two companies that care deeply about new Australian theatre, sharing a space with decades of creative history behind it and plenty more to come.

At Belvoir we gather the best theatre artists we can find, emerging and established, to realise an annual season of works – new works, both Australian and international, reimagined classics and a lasting commitment to Indigenous stories. Audiences remember many landmark productions including *Counting and Cracking, The Drover's Wife, Angels in America, Brothers Wreck, The Glass Menagerie, Neighbourhood Watch, The Wild Duck, Medea, The Diary of a Madman, Death of a Salesman, The Blind Giant is Dancing, Hamlet, Cloudstreet, Aliwa, The Book of Everything, Keating!, The Exile Trilogy, Exit the King, The Sapphires, Faith Healer, FANGIRLS, The Jungle and the Sea* and many more.

Today, under Artistic Director Eamon Flack and Executive Director Aaron Beach, Belvoir tours nationally and internationally, and continues to create its own brand of rough magic for new generations of audiences. We are proud to be creating work that speaks to life and experience in Australia and abroad, continuing our commitment to deliver diverse stories to diverse audiences. Belvoir receives government support for its activities from the federal government through the Australia Council and the state government through Create NSW. We also receive philanthropic and corporate support, which we greatly appreciate and welcome.

BELVOIR ST THEATRE

Gadigal Country
25 Belvoir St, Surry Hills, NSW 2010
belvoir.com.au

CONTACT

Box Office: +61 (2) 9699 3444
Administration: +61 (2) 9698 3344
mail@belvoir.com.au

BELVOIR ST THEATRE STAFF

DIRECTORS

Artistic Director
Eamon Flack

Executive Director
Aaron Beach

ARTISTIC & PROGRAMMING

Artistic Associate
Tom Wright

Resident Director
Hannah Goodwin

Resident Artist
Margaret Thanos

Literary Associate
Ayah Tayeh

Andrew Cameron Fellow
Mehhma Mahli

Balnaves Foundation Fellow
Hannah Belanszky
Bianca Hunt

PRODUCING

Head of Producing
Simone Parrott

Producer
Brittany Santargia

Producer
Emma Diaz

Producer
Emma Sampson

Artistic Administrator
Kelsey Martin

EA & ADMINISTRATION

Executive Assistant
Danielle Green

EDUCATION

Head of Education
Jane May

Education Coordinator
Nicola Denton

PRODUCTION

Head of Production
Tristan Ellis-Windsor

Production Manager
Ren Kenward

Deputy Production Manager
Dana Spence

Resident Stage Manager
Luke McGettigan

Costume Supervisor
Belinda Crawford

Technical Coordinator
Cameron Russell

Construction Manager
Darran Whatley

Leading Hand
Jonas Trovato

MARKETING & CUSTOMER SERVICE

Deputy Executive Director, Marketing, Community & People
Fiona Hulton

Box Office Manager
Natalie Elliot

CRM and Insights Manager
Jason Lee

Ticketing Systems Specialist & CRM Administrator
Tanya Ginori-Cairns

Box Office Coordinator
Lily Emerson

Marketing Manager
Laura Wallace

Digital Content Coordinator
Breanna Macey

Communications Administrator
Jessica Shoppee

Front of House Manager
Alison Benstead

PUBLICITY

Kabuku PR

DEVELOPMENT

Head of Development
Bernie Witham

Partnerships & Grants Coordinator
Lily O'Harte

Philanthropy Administrator
Ellen Harvey

FINANCE & OPERATIONS

Chief Financial Officer
Ash Rathod

Management Accountant
Jay Purohit

Financial Accountant
Dev Solanki

Finance Administrator
Shyleja Paul

BELVOIR ST THEATRE

Gadigal Country
25 Belvoir St, Surry Hills, NSW 2010
belvoir.com.au

CONTACT

Box Office: +61 (2) 9699 3444
Administration: +61 (2) 9698 3344
mail@belvoir.com.au

GRIFFIN DONORS

Income from Griffin activities covers less than 40% of our operating costs—leaving an ever-increasing gap for us to fill through government funding, sponsorship and the generosity of our individual supporters. Your support helps us bridge the gap and keep ticket prices affordable and our work at its best.

To make a donation and a difference, contact Griffin on **(02) 9332 1052** *or donate online at* **griffintheatre.com.au/support**

PROGRAM PATRONS

Griffin Ambassadors
Robertson Foundation

Griffin Amplify
Girgensohn Foundation

Griffin Literary Associate
Malcolm Robertson Foundation
Robertson Foundation

Griffin Redraft Fund
Shane & Cathryn Brennan

Suzie Miller Award
Suzie Miller

Griffin Studio
Gil Appleton
Darin Cooper Foundation
Corinne & Bryan
Kiong Lee & Richard Funston
Malcolm Robertson Foundation
Pip Rath & Wayne Lonergan
Geoff & Wendy Simpson AM
Danielle Smith & Sean Carmody

Griffin Studio Workshop
Shane & Cathryn Brennan (Patron)
Mary Ann Rolfe (Founding Patron)
Iolanda Capodanno
& Juergen Krufczyk
Darin Cooper Foundation
Corinne & Bryan
Bob & Chris Ernst
Jane-Maree Hurley
Susan MacKinnon
Jake Shavikin
Merilyn Sleigh & Raoul de Ferranti

Griffin Women's Initiative
Nicole Abadee
Katrina Barter
Simon Burke AO
Julieanne Campbell
Iolanda Capodanno
Jane Clifford
Jennifer Darin
Eveline Dowling
Mandy Foley
Nicola Forrest AO
Melinda Graham
Sherry Gregory
Rosemary Hannah
& Lynette Preston
Jane-Maree Hurley
Tessa Leong
Susan MacKinnon
Suzie Miller
Naomi Parry
Julia Pincus
Ruth Ritchie
Lenore Robertson AM
Ann Sloan
Deanne Weir
Simone Whetton
Anonymous (1)

PRODUCTION PARTNERS 2025

Naturism **by Ang Collins**
Darin Cooper Foundation
Robert Dick & Erin Shiel
Mandy Foley
Rosemary Hannah
& Lynette Preston
Kate Morgan
Bruce Meagher & Greg Waters
Julia Pincus & Ian Learmonth

SEASON DONORS

Company Patrons $100,000+
Shane & Cathryn Brennan
Neilson Foundation

Season Patrons $50,000-$99,999
Malcolm Robertson Foundation
Robertson Foundation

Mainstage Donors $20,000-$49,999
Darin Cooper Foundation
Girgensohn Foundation
Rosemary Hannah
& Lynette Preston
Suzie Miller
Julia Pincus & Ian Learmonth
Sally Breen Family Foundation
Anonymous (1)

Production Donors $10,000-$19,999
Jenny Ainsworth
Carla Zampatti Foundation
Robert Dick & Erin Shiel
Doc Ross Family Foundation
Gordon & Marie Esden
Mandy Foley
Ingrid Kaiser
Bruce Meagher & Greg Waters
Kate Morgan
Mountain Air Foundation
Rebel Penfold-Russell OAM
Geoff & Wendy Simpson AM
The Skrzynski Foundation
The Wales Family Foundation
The WeirAnderson Foundation

Rehearsal Donors $5,000–$9,999
Brian Abel & Mark Manton
Antoinette Albert
Gil Appleton
Melissa Ball
Lisa Barker & Don Russell
Simon Burke AO
Margaret & Bernard Coles KC
Corinne & Bryan
Bob & Chris Ernst
Stephen Fitzgerald
Carrillo Gantner AC & Ziyin Gantner
Danny Gilbert AM & Kathleen Gilbert
Elizabeth Hurst
Lambert Bridge Foundation
Kiong Lee & Richard Funston
Polese Foundation
Pip Rath & Wayne Lonergan
Seaborn, Broughton & Walford Foundation
Merilyn Sleigh & Raoul de Ferranti
Danielle Smith & Sean Carmody

Final Draft Donors $3,000–$4,999
Baly Douglass Foundation
Iolanda Capodanno
& Juergen Krufczyk
Sherry Gregory
John Head
Jane-Maree Hurley
Susan MacKinnon
Anthony Paull

GRIFFIN DONORS

Workshop Donors $1,000–$2,999
Nicole Abadee & Rob Macfarlan
Emily Aitken
Katrina Barter
Cherry & Peter Best
Ellen Borda
Helen Bowden
Stephen & Annabelle Burley
Julieanne Campbell
Anna Cleary
Jane Clifford
Max Dingle OAM
Eveline Dowling
Ari Droga
Toby Duffy
Brian Everingham
John & Libby Fairfax
Nicholas & Rowena Falzon
Sandra & Rupert Ferman
Sandra Forbes
Melinda Graham
Peter Graves Canberra
Reg Graycar
Mink Greene
Lisa Hamilton & Rob White
Kate Harrison
Libby Higgin & Gae Anderson
Mark Hopkinson & Michelle Opie
David Hoskins & Paul McKnight
Susan Hyde
Colleen Kane
Adrienne & David Kitching
Tessa Leong
John Lewis
Helen Lochhead AO
Patricia Lynch
Matthew & Josephine
Sandra & Kent McPhee
Naomi Parry
Ian Phipps
Andrew Post & Susan Quill
Kate Richardson & Chris Marrable
Steve Riethoff
In memory of Katherine Robertson
Sylvia Rosenblum
Jake Shavikin
Jann Skinner
Ann & Quinn Sloan
Geoffrey Starr
Arahni Sont
Leslie Stern
Martyn Thompson
Sue Thomson
Samantha Turley & Diego Silva
Janet Wahlquist
Richard Weinstein
& Richard Benedict
Simone Whetton
Anonymous (7)

Reading Donors $500–$999
Sally Beath
Alex Bowen & Catherine Sullivan
Alex Bryant-Smith
Jane Christensen
Nick & Carol Dettmann
Elizabeth Evatt
Erica Gray
Susi Hamilton
James Hartwright & Kerrin D'Arcy
Michael Jackson
Noella Lopez
Robert Marks
Simon Marrable
Christopher Matthies
& Graham Parsons
Siobahn Mullany
Jenni Neary AM
Belinda Piggott & David Ojerholm
Virginia Pursell
A.O. Redmond
Steph Sands
Patricia Spinks
Adam Suckling
Fiona Thomas
Stuart Thomas
Michael Thompson OAM & Ian Kelly
Duncan Thomson
Julie Whitfield
Anonymous (4)

First Draft Donors $200-$499
Robyn Ayres
Edwina Birch
Caitlin Brass
David Caulfield
Sue Clark
Edward Cooper & Daniel Zucker
Joanne Court
Brendan Crotty
Bryan Cutler
Melita Daru
Rosemary Dermody
Peter & Lou Duerden
Paul & Jean Eagar
Kevin Farmer
Yvonne Fetherston
R Furley
Deane Golding
Peter Gray & Helen Thwaites
Wendy Gray
Sue Halloran & Jim Allen
Matthew Huxtable
Marian & Nabeel Ibrahim
David Lacey
Bronwyn Leece
Liz Locke
George & Maruschka Loupis
Duncan McKay
Dr Stephen McNamara
Margaret Murphy
Dian Neligan
Carolyn Newman
Sally Patten
Peter Pezzutti
Meredith Phelps
Nick Read
Ann Rocca
Michael & Noelleen Rosen
David Russell
Kevin & Shirley Ryan
Erandi Samarakoon
Jane S
Margaret Teh
Rosemary White
Yoda & Modgie
William Zappa
Ray Ziesing
Anonymous (14)

Griffin Friends Forever
We remember and honour those who have generously supported the future of Australian storytelling through a bequest to Griffin Theatre Company.

Thank you:
Annette Mary Lunney
Estate of the Late John William Roe

CURRENT AS OF 7 JAN 2026

GRIFFIN SPONSORS

Griffin would like to thank the following:

OUR PARTNERS

GOVERNMENT SUPPORTERS

PATRON

LEGACY BENEFACTOR

VENUE PARTNER

CREATIVE PARTNERS

SUSU STUDIO

GIRGENSOHN
FOUNDATION

ROBERTSON FOUNDATION

COMPANY PARTNERS

bourke street bakery

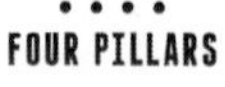

Griffin Theatre Company is assisted by the Australian Government through Creative Australia, its principal arts investment and advisory body.
Griffin Theatre Company is supported by the NSW Government through Create NSW.